JOURNAL FOR THE STUDY OF THE OLD TESTAMENT
SUPPLEMENT SERIES
282

Sheffield Academic Press

'Hannah's Desire, God's Design ,

Early Interpretations of the Story of Hannah

Joan E. Cook

Journal for the Study of the Old Testament
Supplement Series 282

Copyright © 1999 Sheffield Academic Press

Published by
Sheffield Academic Press Ltd
Mansion House
19 Kingfield Road
Sheffield S11 9AS
England

Typeset by Sheffield Academic Press
and
Printed on acid-free paper in Great Britain
by Bookcraft Ltd
Midsomer Norton, Bath

British Library Cataloguing in Publication Data

A catalogue record for this book is available
from the British Library

ISBN 1-85075-909-X

CONTENTS

ACKNOWLEDGMENTS

The efforts and support of many colleagues and friends have made this book possible. Professor Walter Harrelson offered wise and cordial mentoring as I wrote the dissertation that led to this project; St Bonaventure University provided research grants and summer fellowships; the members of the Eastern Great Lakes Biblical Society and the Catholic Biblical Association Task Force on Feminist Hermeneutics offered a valuable critique of my ideas; the Benedictine Sisters in the Studium community at St Benedict Monastery, St Joseph, MN, extended gracious hospitality; Ruth Graf, RSM, offered ongoing comment and enouragement; Theresa Shaffer located countless bibliographic materials; Sally Bolger formatted the manuscript and Lauren de la Vars offered invaluable editing. Special thanks to my Religious Congregation, the Sisters of Charity of Cincinnati, and particularly my small group, who make possible a life of scholarly service.

The study is an outgrowth of my PhD dissertation, 'The Song of Hannah: Text and Contexts' (Vanderbilt University, 1989). In addition, several other earlier works influenced this project, and have appeared elsewhere. There are 'Pseudo-Philo's Song of Hannah: Testament of a Mother in Israel', *JSP* 9 (1991), pp. 103-114; 'Females and the Feminine in Pseudo-Philo', in *Proceedings: Eastern Great Lakes and Midwest Biblical Societies* 13 (1993), pp. 151-59; 'The Song of Hannah in Pseudo-Philo's Biblical Antiquities', in M. Kiley (ed.), *Prayer from Alexander to Constantine: A Critical Anthology* (New York: Routledge, 1997), pp. 73-78; and 'Hannah's Later Songs: A Study in Comparative Methods of Interpretation', in C.A. Evans and J.A. Sanders (eds.), *Early Christian Interpretations of the Scriptures of Israel: Investigations and Proposals* (JSNTSup, 148; SSEJC, 5; Sheffield: Sheffield Academic Press, 1998), pp. 241-61

This book is dedicated to my sister, Martha Went, her husband Bob and their son Andy, who gave their son and brother back to God; and to the memory of my nephew, Anthony Joseph Went (1972–97). Tony showed us how to live with eagerness and gratitude.

ABBREVIATIONS

AB	Anchor Bible
ANET	James B. Pritchard (ed.), *Ancient Near Eastern Texts Relating to the Old Testament* (Princeton, NJ: Princeton University Press, 3rd edn with Supplement, 1969)
Ant.	Flavius Josephus, *The Antiquities of the Jews*
AusBR	*Australian Biblical Review*
BDB	F. Brown, S.R. Driver and C.A. Briggs, *A Hebrew and English Lexicon of the Old Testament* (Oxford: Clarendon Press, 1951)
BibInt	*Biblical Interpretation: A Journal of Contemporary Approaches*
Gen. Rab.	*Genesis Rabbah*
HTR	*Harvard Theological Review*
ICC	International Critical Commentary
JBL	*Journal of Biblical Literature*
JETS	*Journal of the Evangelical Theological Society*
JJS	*Journal of Jewish Studies*
JSNTSup	*Journal for the Study of the New Testament*, Supplement Series
JSOTSup	*Journal for the Study of the Old Testament*, Supplement Series
JSP	*Journal for the Study of the Pseudepigrapha*
JTS	*Journal of Theological Studies*
KAT	Kommentar zum Alten Testament
NCB	New Century Bible
NRSV	New Revised Standard Version
OBT	Overtures to Biblical Theology
OTL	Old Testament Library
OTP	James Charlesworth (ed.), *Old Testament Pseudepigrapha*
RHPR	*Revue d'histoire et de philosophie religieuses*
SBL	Society of Biblical Liturature
SBLDS	SBL Dissertation Series
SJOT	*Scandinavian Journal of the Old Testament*
SNTSMS	Society for New Testament Studies Monograph Series
SSEJC	Studies in Scripture in Early Judaism and Christianitry
ZAW	*Zeitschrift für die alttestamentliche Wissenschaft*

Chapter 1

INTRODUCTION

This study analyzes the biblical personage Hannah as a literary entity, to illustrate her unique significance in the traditions of Israel. As mother of Samuel and teacher of all Israel she is the catalyst for reform of the priesthood and creation of the monarchy. To achieve that end I will develop three interweaving themes: first, the literary issue of the barren mother type scene; second, the theological theme of divine guidance and human initiative; and third, the historical question of early biblical interpretation.

I will discuss the Hannah materials in four works: 1 Samuel 1–2 and then three later appropriations: in Pseudo-Philo's (*Ps.-Philo*) *Biblical Antiquities* (*Bib. Ant.*), *Targum of the Prophets* (*Targ. Neb.*), and Luke's Infancy Narrative in Luke 1–2. These three selections were easily made because *Biblical Antiquities* and *Targ. Neb.* refer explicitly to Hannah and include a version of the biblical account. And Luke's Infancy Narrative clearly alludes to the Hannah account in several ways. These three appropriations are atypical, however. Very few expanded Bibles and later appropriations mention Hannah at all, and then only briefly. Many early retellings of the biblical stories omit her altogether, or include her without naming her. For instance, the book of Sirach includes Samuel in its praise of ancestors in chs. 44–50, but does not mention Hannah, or any women at all (Sir. 44.1–50.21). And Josephus refers to her, offering a summary of the biblical account. It shifts the scene at the shrine, having Hannah tell Eli she is praying for children, after which Eli blesses her with the assurance that her prayer will be answered. But it omits Hannah's words, including the Song (*Ant.* 5.10 §§2–3).

The study proceeds as follows. In this chapter I discuss several introductory concepts and themes. First I consider the biblical type of the barren mother in general, then look closely at the three models of the

type. Next I introduce the theme of divine and human initiative in relation to the barren mother stories, to highlight Hannah's unique position
and actions from that perspective. Then I discuss general characteristics
of early biblical interpretation, to introduce the later versions and
appropriations of the Hannah narrative.

Chapter 2 considers the biblical Hannah story in some detail: its plot,
relation to the barren mother type, and unique literary features, to highlight Hannah's uniqueness among the biblical barren mothers and her
initiative in relation to the Deity.

Chapter 3 takes up the discussion of *Pseudo-Philo*'s *Biblical Antiquities* Particular to that version of the story are its private and public
aspects which form two separate plots that eventually merge into one,
women in *Biblical Antiquities* and the motif of love in the story.

Then Chapter 4 discusses the Hannah story in *Targum of the
Prophets*. It focuses almost entirely on the Song because the narrative
itself is exactly the same as in the biblical story.

Chapter 5 analyzes Luke's Infancy Narrative, in particular its dual
adaptation of the Hannah story and its complex rendering of the barren
mother type.

Chapter 6 summarizes the portrayals of Hannah, then analyzes the
shifts in her characterization and role throughout the later appropriations in order to highlight the development of the three themes: the
barren mother type scene, divine guidance and human initiative, and
early biblical interpretation. It then offers suggestions for contemporary
resignification of the stories.

The Barren Mother Type

The lens through which this study considers Hannah is the barren
mother type scene. A look at the type illustrates its particular characteristics. The biblical type of the barren mother involves a childless
woman who bears a son through divine intervention, then takes steps to
insure her son's success. Often the sons in question serve a special
function as leaders of the people in times of crisis or transition (e.g.
Isaac, Jacob, Joseph, Samuel).[1] The Deity acts not only in the particular
event of childbearing, but also on a larger scale in fulfillment of divine
promises to Israel.

---

1. P. Trible, *God and the Rhetoric of Sexuality* (OBT; Philadelphia: Fortress
Press, 1978), pp. 34-35.

In addition to Hannah (1 Sam. 1.1–2.21), several other women are childless: Sarah (Gen. 11.29-30; 16.1–18.15; 21.1-8), Rebekah (Gen. 25.20-34; 26.34–27.45), Rachel (Gen. 29.15–30.24), Samson's mother (Judg. 13.2-25), the Shunammite woman (2 Kgs 4.8-37), and the woman in Ezra's vision (2 Esd. 9.38–10.54). These women share a lack of blame for their childlessness, in contrast to others whose barrenness is described as punishment (e.g. Gen. 20.17-18; Lev. 20.20-21; 2 Sam. 6.23; Job 18.19; Isa. 14.22; Hos. 9.10-18).[2]

Actually, the Bible does not specifically call Hannah barren (עקרה), but states simply, 'Hannah had no children' (לחנה אין ילדים, 1 Sam. 1.2), because 'the Lord had closed her womb' (vv. 5-6), suggesting divine action.[3] The only other appearance of the expression 'the Lord had closed her womb' occurs with regard to Abimelech's wives and female slaves, 'For the Lord had closed all the wombs of the house of Abimelech because of Sarah, Abraham's wife' (Gen. 20.18). In this case the closed wombs represent punishment of Abimelech and protection of the promise to Abraham.

In contrast, most of the other barren mother narratives refer to the woman as עקרה: Sarai (Gen. 11.30), Rebekah (25.2), Rachel (29.3), and Samson's mother (Judg. 13.2). The Vulgate refers to the woman in Ezra's vision as *sterilis* (2 Esd. 9.43), the same word with which it translates עקרה in the above texts. And the Song of Hannah praises the Lord because 'the barren woman (עקרה) bears seven' (1 Sam. 2.5). But regarding the Shunammite woman the text reads simply, 'She has no son' (בן אין־לה, 2 Kgs 4.14). No explanation for her childlessness is given.

---

2. M. Callaway, *Sing, O Barren One: A Study in Comparative Midrash* (SBLDS, 91; Atlanta: Scholars Press, 1986), pp. 16-17.

3. All quotations from the Bible are from NRSV unless otherwise indicated. The text is problematic at this point. The conjunction כי following the unexplainable word אפס can be rendered either as causative or concessive. In addition, the absence of the competition element from the LXX narrative compounds the problem and reinforces the likelihood that MT and LXX descended from different *Vorlagen*. I follow MT; see J.E. Cook, 'The Song of Hannah: Text and Contexts' (Vanderbilt University dissertation, 1989), p. 66. See also Callaway, *Sing*, pp. 44-46; P.K. McCarter, Jr, *I Samuel: A New Translation with Introduction, Notes and Commentary* (AB, 8; Garden City, NY: Doubleday, 1980), pp. 51-52; S.D. Walters, 'Hannah and Anna: The Greek and Hebrew Texts of 1 Samuel 1', *JBL* 107 (1988), pp. 385-412 (388-97).

The distinctive wording in the Hannah narrative might imply punishment by association with Abimelech's house. But it also focuses on a divine purpose with regard to Hannah. It foreshadows both Hannah's initiative in this regard and divine intervention on her behalf and in the interest of the promise. Because the narrative tension is introduced around the motif of childlessness I analyze the Hannah narrative within the type of the barren mother.

Each of the women bears a son through divine intervention. In Sarah's case God promises the child to Abraham. Isaac prays to the Lord for a child for Rebekah, and the Lord answers. Rachel bears Joseph when God remembers her. Samson's mother receives a promise from the angel of the Lord that she will bear a son. Hannah bears a son when the Lord remembers her. The Shunammite woman is promised by Elisha, who is identified as a man of God, that she will bear a son. And the woman in Ezra's vision bears a child when God hears her prayer. These interventions occur in different ways according to the three models of the type. The variations become evident in the discussion of the three models.

Thirdly, in the barren mother type the mother takes steps to ensure her son's success. Sarah insists that Hagar and Ishmael leave her household (Gen. 21.8-21) to protect Isaac's inheritance, and Rebekah arranges for Jacob rather than Esau to receive their father Isaac's blessing (27.1-29). Rachel's efforts on behalf of Joseph are less direct. She steals her father Laban's household gods when Jacob and his family prepare to leave Laban's house (31.19), mocking his beliefs and retaliating for his trickery of his two daughters. After Rachel's premature death, Jacob assumes the maternal care of Joseph. He makes him a 'long robe with sleeves' because he loves Joseph more than his other sons (Gen. 37.3). Samson's mother tries to convince him to marry a Danite rather than a Philistine, but her efforts prove unsuccessful (Judg. 14.3). Hannah gives Samuel to the service of the Lord under Eli's care (1 Sam. 1.25-28). On her annual pilgrimage to Shiloh she takes him a little robe to wear (2.19). The Shunammite woman goes to Elisha and pleads on her son's behalf when the son dies (2 Kgs 4.22-37). And the woman in Ezra's vision cares for her son and arranges his marriage (2 Esd. 9.46-47). The mothers' efforts on their sons' behalf demonstrate their ongoing concern for the well-being and future of their offspring.[4]

4.   J.G. Williams notes the appearance of the 'arche-mother as mediating agent' within several birth narratives. The woman in each case protects either her

Most of the sons serve as leaders during pivotal times of crisis or transition. Isaac protects the divine promise of offspring to Abraham. He prays for his barren wife Rebekah (Gen. 25.21) and secures land and water for his household (ch. 26). He is tricked into giving his blessing to Jacob (27.1-29), but then sends him to find a wife from among his mother's people (28.1-5), assuring the continuation of the promise into the next generation.

Jacob likewise protects the promise. Through complicity with his mother he receives his father's blessing (Gen. 27.1-29), marries Laban's daughters Leah and Rachel (29.15-28), flees from Laban with his family and livestock (31.1-42), takes steps to dissipate the enmity between Esau and himself (32.3–33.17), and arranges for his family to subsist in time of drought by relocating them to Egypt (ch. 46).

Rachel's son Joseph serves as head of pharaoh's household, assuring in the long run that his family will prosper in Egypt (41.40). Samson's actions are the antithesis of a leader's until he destroys the Philistine lords by toppling their house (Judg. 17.28-30). Samuel works to establish the Israelite monarchy by negotiating between the people and God and by anointing Saul and David (1 Sam. 8; 10.1; 16.13).

On another level the barren mother stories serve as chapters in the ongoing story of divine guidance to Israel. This aspect of the type will be discussed later in the chapter, in the context of divine and human initiatives.

husband or her son from another, hostile male. Sarah protects Abraham from foreign rulers (Sarai in Gen. 12.11-20 and Sarah in ch. 20) and Isaac from sharing his inheritance with Ishmael (21.9-14); Rebekah arranges for Jacob, rather than Esau, to receive Isaac's blessing (ch. 27). Rachel helps Jacob trick Laban during their getaway (31.17-35). Moses receives help from three women: his mother takes steps to save him from Pharaoh's order of death as a newborn; Pharaoh's daughter finds the infant Moses and arranges for his care (Exod. 2.1-10); Moses' wife saves him from divine wrath by circumcising him (4.24-26). Hannah dissipates Eli's interference (1 Sam. 1.13-18) and Elkanah's attempt to give up Samuel too soon (vv. 22-23). See his *Women Recounted: Narrative Thinking and the God of Israel* (Sheffield: Almond Press, 1982), pp. 55-58. J.C. Exum points out in this regard the protection not only of the man but also of the promise in her 'Mother in Israel: A Familiar Story Reconsidered', in L. Russell (ed.), *Feminist Interpretation of the Bible* (Philadelphia: Westminster Press, 1985), pp. 73-85 (79-82).

Barren Mother Models

All the stories in the type contain the same basic elements. But
additional details emerge when the type is subdivided into three
models.[5]

The first model, competition, includes five elements: a favored wife
is childless; her husband has another, rival woman; the rival bears a son
for her husband; the rival belittles the childless wife, causing conflict;
the childless wife bears a son through divine intervention; and the child
receives a significant name.[6] This model characterizes the stories of
Sarah, Rachel and Hannah.

The second model, the promise, also includes five elements: the wife
is childless; a messenger from God appears to one or the other spouse;

---

5.   R. Alter refers to the type as the 'annunciation' and includes the two models
within it in his *The Art of Biblical Narrative* (New York: Basic Books, 1981),
pp. 49, 85. J.G. Williams divides the 'arche-mother' type into 'contest of the barren
wife' and 'promise' models, *Women Recounted*, pp. 48-55. A. Brenner refers only
to the general type, which she calls 'hero's mother' in *The Israelite Woman: Social
Role and Literary Type in Biblical Narrative* (Sheffield: JSOT Press, 1985), pp. 92-
95. Her treatment provides a general overview, but does not permit the examination
of significant details that a more nuanced study allows. Exum, 'Mother', concen-
trates on the competition model in order to focus on the matriarchs as recipients of
divine intervention. They function in the narrative to move the plot forward, and in
Israel's history to move the promise toward fulfillment, pp. 75-76. E. Fuchs
identifies only the general type, 'annunciation', noting that the woman's role varies
and 'constitute(s) a consistently increasing emphasis on the potential mother as the
true heroine', in 'The Literary Characterization of Mothers and Sexual Politics in
the Hebrew Bible', in A.Y. Collins (ed.), *Feminist Perspectives on Biblical Scholarship* (Chico, CA: Scholars Press, 1985), pp. 117-36 (119). R.K. Gnuse proposes a
variation of the promise model, calling it a 'birth announcement'. It includes three
elements: declaration of the coming birth, designation of the son's name and
indication of his future role. He suggests that Hannah deviates from the type in his
The Dream Theophany of Samuel (Lanham, MD: University Press of America,
1984), pp. 179-80. As I see it, this delineation supports my understanding of
Hannah as a reversal of, rather than deviation from, the particular features of the
model.

6.   Brenner's delineation of the type emphasizes the rivals' need for each other
as a significant reason for their competition, *Israelite Woman*, pp. 93-95. J.G.
Williams delineates the characteristics of this model except that he calls all the
women 'barren', *Women Recounted*, pp. 48-49. I prefer 'childless' in keeping with
the Hebrew text.

the messenger promises a son; the event is confirmed despite human doubt; and the promised son is born and receives a significant name.[7] These elements appear in the accounts of Sarah, Samson's mother, Hannah, and the Shunammite woman.

The third model, the request, involves a simpler plot with only three elements: someone requests a son for a barren wife; the Lord hears the request; and a son is given. The accounts of Rebekah, Rachel, Hannah, and the woman in Ezra's vision contain these elements.[8]

Childless Women in Relation to the Models

A look at the details on the various stories highlights their adherence to the different models.

Competition Stories
First, the Sarah, Rachel and Hannah accounts involve competition and contain the elements mentioned above. All three childless women are the husband's favorite. In Sarah's case she is Abraham's wife whom he favors above her maid Hagar; Rachel and Hannah are the wives their husbands love, rather than their other wives Leah and Peninnah.

In each case the other woman bears a son: Hagar bears Ishmael (interestingly, this happens at Sarai's instigation); Leah bears four sons whom the Lord gives her because she is hated; and Peninnah has children about whom no details are given.

The rival belittles the childless wife, causing conflict. In fact, Sarah and Hagar engage in two conflicts: the first occurs before the Lord renames Sarai, when Hagar conceives by Abram, then looks on Sarai with contempt. Consequently Sarai deals harshly with her, until Hagar flees, then returns at the angel's requests. The second conflict occurs

---

7.   J.G. Williams again calls all the women 'barren' and has the messenger appear to the woman. I prefer the more general statement: Abraham rather than Sarah receives the promise and Hannah makes rather than receives it. Samson's mother and the Shunammite woman are the only two who actually receive the promise. J.G. Williams, *Women Recounted*, p. 52.

8.   By delineating this model as distinct from the other two I emphasize the initiatives taken by the women in pursuit of divine favor. J.G. Williams includes initiative as part of the competition model, where he notes the efforts of Sarai, Rachel, and Hannah. But his explanation refers to the women's competitive tactics vis-à-vis their rivals rather than to their actual requests for offspring. J.G. Williams, *Women Recounted*, pp. 49-52.

when the renamed Sarah and Abraham's (17.5, 15) son Isaac is weaned: Sarah prevails on Abraham to banish Hagar and Ishmael rather than allow Ishmael to play with her son Isaac (21.9-14). At that point the stakes are higher: Sarah works to protect her son of promise from possible competition with her rival's son over questions of inheritance.

The conflict is strongest between Rachel and Leah, but it begins with an indirect provocation: Leah gives her first four sons names that express her desire for her husband's love. For example, she names her first-born Reuben, saying, 'because the Lord has looked on my affliction; surely now my husband will love me'. She calls her third son Levi, which she interprets, 'Now this time my husband will be joined to me because I have borne him three sons.'[9] Rachel envies Leah and gives her maid to Jacob, then Leah does likewise; then the two women fight over the mandrakes; when Rachel bears Joseph she names him with the request, 'May the Lord add to me another son' (29.30–30.24).

But in Hannah's case the competition is one-sided, even though three people belittle her. Rival Peninnah torments Hannah every year at the annual festival at Shiloh; Hannah is distressed, but does not respond to Peninnah's teasing (1 Sam. 1.6-7). Hannah's husband trivializes her anguish with his uncomprehending questions, to which she does not respond. The priest Eli belittles Hannah; he mistakes her praying lips as a sign of drunkenness. She does respond to Eli but tells him only that she is praying to YHWH from her trouble and anxiety (1.13-17); no tormenting of Eli by Hannah takes place.[10]

Finally, in the competition stories the childless wife bears a son through divine intervention and he receives a significant name. The Lord visits Sarah, who bears Isaac. Abraham gives him the name and Sarah interprets it 'God has brought laughter for me; everyone who hears will laugh with me' (Gen 21.1-3, 6); the Deity remembers Rachel and she bears Joseph, 'God has taken away my reproach' (30.22-23),

---

9. Callaway, *Sing*, pp. 26-28.

10. Brenner notes that competing wives complement each other to such an extent that the two together equal conflicting sides of the same coin, *Israelite Woman*, pp. 92-94. But Hannah's uninvolvement in competition against Peninnah and her direct steps to accomplish her purpose give her a more independent status than Brenner's characterization permits. Peninnah does, however, function as a foil for Hannah: the taunting rival highlights Hannah's straightforward simplicity and dignity. A. Berlin, *Poetics and Interpretation of Biblical Narrative* (Sheffield: Almond Press, 1983), p. 136.

and later Benjamin. 'And as her soul was departing (for she died), she called his name Benoni; but his father called his name Benjamin' (35.18); likewise the Lord remembers Hannah, who bears Samuel and interprets his name 'I have asked him of the Lord' (1 Sam. 1.19-20).

Promise Stories

The promise model describes the stories of Sarah, Samson's mother, Hannah, and the Shunammite woman. In each case a messenger from God appears, promises a son and confirms the promise in spite of human doubt; the son is born and receives a significant name.

In Sarah's case Abraham rather than Sarah receives not just one but three promises: first, the Lord promises Abram before the names are changed, 'your own son shall be your heir' (Gen. 15.4). Then the Lord promises more specifically, 'As for Sarai your wife, you shall not call her name Sarai, but Sarah shall be her name. I will bless her, and moreover I will give you a son by her; I will bless her, and she shall be a mother of nations; kings of peoples shall come from her' (17.15-19). Abraham laughs his doubt, and the Lord repeats the promise with instructions to name the child Isaac.

Then three visitors, one of whom turns out to be the Lord, makes the same promise to Abraham within Sarah's earshot.[11] Sarah, from her position in the tent, hears the three assure Abraham that she will bear a son. Her fearful laugh because of her age affronts the divine power, but the Lord repeats the promise (18.9-15).[12]

The Lord also gives a promise to Sarah's rival Hagar: she will have many descendants and will bear a son to be named Ishmael. Hagar is amazed, not at the promise, but that she has seen the Lord and lived (16.7-13).

In the account of Samson's mother, 'The angel of the Lord appeared to the woman and said to her, "Behold, you are barren and have no children; but you shall conceive and bear a son...the boy shall be a nazirite from birth, and he shall begin to deliver Israel from the hand of

---

11. See G. von Rad's explanation of this troublesome reference to three men, then to the singular YHWH, in connection with his discussion of hospitality in the ancient Near East in *Genesis: A Commentary* (OTL; Philadelphia: Westminster Press, rev. edn, 1973), pp. 204-206. And Callaway notes 'reward for hospitality' features of the narrative in *Sing*, pp. 18-19.

12. Moreover, YHWH has the last laugh, as the child's name suggests; J.G. Williams, *Women Recounted*, p. 53.

the Philistines"' (Judg. 13.3, 5). Her husband Manoah is the one to question the message, and the messenger confirms the promise, except for Samson's destined role in Israel's life. When Samson is born his mother names him, but no explanation is given for the name.[13]

In the third promise story Hannah reverses the promise element: she herself makes the paradoxical promise to give back to the Lord the son for whom she prays: 'She vowed a vow and said, "O Lord of hosts, if thou wilt indeed look on the affliction of thy maidservant, and remember me, and not forget thy maidservant, but wilt give to thy maidservant a son, then I will give him to the Lord all the days of his life, and no razor shall, touch his head"' (1 Sam. 1.11).

This time Eli expresses doubt by questioning her actions and interpreting her moving lips as a sign of drunkenness. When she protests he gives unknowing confirmation in the form of a blessing: 'Go in peace, and the God of Israel grant your petition which you have made to him' (1.17).[14] Then 'in due time Hannah conceived and bore a son, and she called his name Samuel, for she said, "I have asked him of the Lord"' (1.20).

In the case of the Shunammite woman, Elisha's servant Gehazi suggests the promise to the prophet as a reward to the woman for her hospitality. She protests, '"No, my lord, O man of God; do not lie to your maidservant". But the woman conceived, and she bore a son about that time the following spring, as Elisha had said to her' (2 Kgs 4.16-17). The son's name is not mentioned in the account.

Request Stories

In the request model someone requests a son for a barren wife, the Lord hears, and gives a son. This applies to Rebekah, Rachel, Hannah and the woman in Ezra's vision. In Rebekah's case it is Isaac who prays, 'And Isaac prayed to the Lord for his wife, because she was barren; and the Lord granted his prayer, and Rebekah his wife conceived' (Gen. 25.21). But even though the story is straightforward at first, it goes on to include elements of competition and promise: Rebekah has no rival

---

13. The narrative diverges from the Genesis accounts by highlighting the woman, even though she remains unnamed, rather than her husband Manoah; Exum, 'Mother', pp. 82-84; Fuchs, 'Characterization', pp. 123-25.

14. Her straightforward response to Eli persuades the priest of her integrity, and his unknowing blessing consoles her; Alter, *Art*, pp. 85-86.

wife, but her sons compete fiercely: they fight from the womb, because of which Rebekah receives a promise from the Lord regarding them. In keeping with the divine promise they compete for the birthright, and she and her husband compete over the issue of the sons' success, especially regarding the blessing. Sarah had worked to assure that Isaac would receive his father's inheritance; now he in turn passes on the blessing to the son whom his mother Rebekah favors.[15]

In the Rachel account, she asks her husband Jacob for a son, 'Give me children, or I shall die!' (30.1). Jacob objects to her casting him in the divine role, and eventually the Lord remembers her and gives her a son whom she names Joseph, implying a request for another son.

In Hannah's case she herself prays for a son. Her request is both public and formal. She makes it at the Shiloh shrine and vows to return to the Lord the son she requests (1 Sam. 1.9-11).[16]

Finally, the woman in Ezra's vision prays 30 years for a son, then the Lord hears and answers her prayer. As she explains to Ezra, 'After thirty years God heard your handmaid, and looked upon my low estate, and considered my distress, and gave me a son' (2 Esd. 9.44-45). Her story ends in tragedy: on her son's wedding night he dies. In fact, when Ezra sees her in his vision, she is grieving for her lost son (9.38-41). The angel Uriel interprets Ezra's vision for him: the woman symbolizes

---

15. Exum, 'Mother', p. 78. Fuchs notes that, although the request came from Isaac rather than Rebekah, the Lord explained the twins' competition to her in response to her inquiry; 'Characterization', p. 122.

16. Hannah's direct request supports Fuchs's idea of the gradually increasing dominance of the women in the type scenes, in 'Characterization', pp. 125-26. In fact, Exum's interpretation of the events surrounding Moses' birth and infancy call attention to Moses' mother's independent resourcefulness and the narrator's silence regarding his father. She made an ark and placed him in it at the river bank to protect him from the death Pharaoh had decreed for newborn Hebrew sons. Then, with the help of her daughter, she received him back from Pharaoh's daughter to nurse (Gen. 1.22–2.10). From Exum's interpretation one can infer additional parallels between Moses and Samuel: both Exod. and 1 Sam. begin with birth narratives in which women's faith impels them to insure their sons' futures (Moses' mother 'gives' him to Pharaoh to rear, thus not only saving Moses' life but in the long run guiding the future of the entire people; and Samuel's mother gives him to the Lord in the person of Eli, setting the stage for Samuel to guide the future of the people). See J.C. Exum, '"You Shall Let Every Daughter Live": A Study of Exodus 1.8–2.10', in M.A. Tolbert (ed.), *The Bible and Feminist Hermeneutics* (Semeia, 28; Atlanta: Scholars Press, 1983), pp. 63-82 (72-82).

Jerusalem, and she grieves because the city was destroyed by the
Romans (10.41-49). But the reward to the faithful in the end time will
far outweigh the sufferings they endure (12.34).

Divine Guidance

The second leg on which this study stands is the ancient understanding
of divine causality. It was the 'cultural assumption of the ancient Near
East that certain occurrences and concatenations of events were
attributable to divine agency'.[17] Divine actions were described as
having motive, deliberation and purpose, which the human authors
embodied in story form. And human response determined whether the
plan would move forward or be thwarted. Human consent would assure
the continuance of the divine plan, while lack of cooperation would
interfere with the plan.

Divine Intervention
In ancient Israel the biblical authors had the task of ascribing all divine
interventions to the one God.[18] Such events in their founding story
included the plagues inflicted on the Egyptians (Exod. 7.14–12.42), the
parting of the Sea of Reeds (ch. 14), and several instances of feeding
the people in the wilderness (e.g. Exod. 16). Later, the Deuteronomistic
historian attributed military defeats to divine punishment for the
people's sins (e.g. the destruction of Israel and Judah at the hands of the
Assyrians and Babylonians).

Within this worldview the Hebrew Bible frequently reports that the
Deity commissioned humans to carry forward the divine work of gov-
erning and protecting the people. This is evident in the call to Moses to
negotiate with the pharaoh the release of the Israelite slaves and the
commissioning of Amos to leave his flocks and sycamore trees and
condemn the injustices of the northern kingdom. It is evident in God's
words to Jeremiah, 'Before you were born I consecrated you; I
appointed you a prophet to the nations' (Jer. 1.5). In fact, the Western
world traces its religious ancestry to the divine charge to Abraham,
called Abram at the time, 'Go from your country and your kindred and
your father's house to the land that I will show you. I will make of you

17. D. Patrick, *The Rendering of God in the Old Testament* (OBT; Philadelphia:
Fortress Press, 1981), p. 79.

18. Patrick, *Rendering*, p. 88.

a great nation, and I will bless you, and make your name great, so that you will be a blessing' (Gen. 12.1-2). These words summarize the beginnings of Western religion. God commissioned Abraham with a task reinforced with the divine promise of blessing. And the religious traditions that flow from that memory all base their beliefs and structures on the foundation of divine initiative on behalf of the people.

Human Initiative
On the other hand, the divine purpose was influenced and even changed by human initiative. For instance Abraham pleaded with God to spare the city of Sodom if 50 righteous people could be found. When God agreed, Abraham gradually reduced the number to be found to 10, to which God responded, 'For the sake of 10 I will not destroy it' (Gen. 18.32). At another time Moses bargained, 'Why should the Egyptians say, "It was with evil intent that he brought them out to kill them in the mountains, and to consume them from the face of the earth"? Turn from your fierce wrath; change your mind and do not bring disaster on your people', and 'the Lord changed his mind about the disaster that he planned to bring on his people' (Exod. 32.12, 14). On another occasion Amos's repeated plea is recorded, 'O Lord God, forgive, I beg you! How can Jacob stand? He is so small!' at which the Lord relented (Amos 7.2-6).

Hannah stands in line with those who influenced the course of history by venturing to influence the divine plan. Her promise to God 'If only you will look on the misery of your servant, and remember me, and not forget your servant, but will give to your servant a male child, then I will set him before you as a consecrated one until the day of his death' (1 Sam. 1.11) resulted in the birth of Samuel, the reform of the priesthood, and the birth of the Israelite monarchy.

Divine Causality in Barren Mother Stories
The ancient belief in divine causality permeates the barren mother stories as well. In fact, the understanding that children are a gift of God offers a backdrop ideally suited for stories of childbearing in spite of apparently impossible odds. They recount specific instances of divine faithfulness to the promises made originally to Abraham, particularly the assurances of descendants and a nation. And the particularities of each story set the stage for unique actions by the Deity on behalf of the community.

Sarah was 90 years old when God promised Abraham a son. Her own and Abraham's laughter attest to their incredulity at the divine announcement (Gen. 17.17; 18.12-13). The birth of Isaac set in motion the promise of many descendants to Abraham and Sarah. Rebekah endured a very difficult pregnancy because her twin sons fought from the start, even in the womb (25.21-23). Rachel bore Joseph when God remembered her and opened her womb (30.22). The births of Jacob and Joseph continued the fulfillment of the divine promise, and they determined the exact line of Abraham's descendants. Samson's mother was barren (Judg. 13.2). She received the messenger's promise that the son to be born to her would 'begin to deliver Israel from the hand of the Philistines' (13.5). When Samson announced his desire to marry a Philistine woman, his parents tried unsuccessfully to dissuade him. But in fact, Samson's marriage was the means by which the Lord delivered Israel (14.4).

Hannah was barren, tormented by her rival wife, and misunderstood by her husband and the priest (1 Sam. 1.6-8, 13-17). Her son Samuel took over the priesthood from Eli's corrupt sons, and later instituted the monarchy. The Shunammite woman's husband was old, and she thought Elisha was deceiving her with his promise of a son (2 Kgs 4.16). Elisha's successful effort to bring the Shunammite son back to life was one of a series of actions that confirmed the divine protection of the people. The woman in Ezra's vision had been married for 30 years, during which she prayed constantly for a child (2 Esd. 9.45). She represented Jerusalem, 'the city of the Most High'; and the events in her son's life represented the joys and sorrows that befell the city. And the vision itself depicted divine actions on behalf of its inhabitants (10.38-59).

And the mothers' efforts to insure their sons' success incarnated divine inbreakings in the lives of the people. Sarah's insistence that Abraham banish Hagar and Ishmael protected her son Isaac from the possibility that Hagar's son Ishmael might receive the inheritance intended for the first-born. And she thus insured that the promise to Abraham would continue through her own son Isaac. Rebekah's arrangement for Jacob to receive his father's blessing upheld the divine promise to her, 'The elder shall serve the younger', and assured that Isaac's line would continue through the younger son (Gen. 25.23). Rachel's efforts on behalf of Joseph were more indirect. She stole her father's household gods and took them along when her husband Jacob left Laban and returned to his own home. The powerless idol was fundamentally worthless, but symbolized Rachel's retaliation for her father's trickery in the marriages of Rachel and her sister Leah (31.19-35).[19]

Samson's marriage was frowned upon by his parents, but nevertheless was the way God delivered Israel from the Philistines (Judg. 14.4). Hannah positioned Samuel at the Shiloh shrine, assuring the divine presence among the people in his priesthood and eventually in the monarchy (1 Sam. 3, 8). The Shunammite woman's insistence that Elisha come to her dead son demonstrated that Elisha acted in the name of the Lord (2 Kgs 4.20-37). And the woman in Ezra's vision reared her son and arranged his marriage. The vision represented hope for the future of Jerusalem (2 Esd. 9.46-47; 10.44-50).

Divine and Human Causality in the Barren Mother Models

Returning to the barren mother type, a review of the models suggests that of the three, only the third (the request) attributes the birth of the child to human initiative. The first (competition) and second (promise) have as their point of departure the divine intervention that makes possible the birth of the child.

Divine Intervention in Competition and Promise Stories
In the case of Sarah, who illustrates both the competition and promise models, the narrative makes clear that the child is the result of divine intervention. God announced to Abraham the coming of the child (Gen. 17.16; 18.14).

Likewise with Rachel in the competition model the narrative specifies in several ways that divine activity makes possible the birth of children. In her case, Jacob exclaimed in response to her plea that he give her a son, 'Am I in the place of God, who has withheld from you the fruit of the womb?' (30.2). And her child was conceived when God remembered her. Rachel acknowledged that Joseph was a divine gift when she said, 'God has taken away my reproach'; and she named him Joseph, saying, 'May the Lord add to me another son!' (30.22-24). Rachel will be discussed again below with regard to the request model.

Samson's mother received a promise from the angel that she would

---

19. C. Westermann, *Genesis 12–36: A Commentary* (trans. J.J. Scullion; Minneapolis: Augsburg, 1985), p. 495.

bear a son (Judg. 13.3). And so did the Shunammite woman, but in less explicit terms. Elisha promised her, 'At this season, in due time, you shall embrace a son'. She replied, 'No, my lord, O man of God; do not deceive your servant' (2 Kgs 4.16). The promise was not explicitly from God, but from Elisha, the man of God who served as divine messenger.

Human Initiative in Request Stories

But unlike the first two models, the request model highlights human initiative. In Rebekah's situation, Isaac asked God for a son. His request is all the more significant considering how seldom Isaac acted throughout the entire narrative. But he did take action to protect the promise: 'Isaac prayed to the LORD for his wife, because she was barren; and the LORD granted his prayer, and his wife Rebekah conceived' (Gen. 25.21).

Rachel asked her husband for children (30.1-2). Hannah prayed for a son, reinforcing her request with a vow (1 Sam. 1.10-11). And the woman in Ezra's vision also asked for a child (2 Esd. 9.43-45).

Of the four women, only Hannah and the woman in Ezra's vision asked God directly for a child, while Rachel asked her husband, and Isaac asked God for a son for himself and Rebekah. And the fact that Hannah is named but not the woman in Ezra's vision further distinguishes her within the type. A closer look shows that Hannah is unique in other ways as well.

Hannah in the Three Models

Hannah is the only barren mother who fits all three models. Her relationship to each of them illustrates the unique tension between divine and human initiative found in her story. In terms of the competition model, the narrative relates that she bore a son through divine intervention when the Lord remembered her (1 Sam. 1.20). And she recalled the divine gift in her interpretation of his name, 'I have asked him of the Lord'.

From the perspective of the promise model, Hannah herself promised at the Shiloh shrine that if her prayer was heard she would give the child back to the Lord (1 Sam. 1.11). Her pledge differs significantly from the other promises in this model insofar as she made it herself: it was not made to her by someone else, nor was it made on her behalf.

Finally, the request model illustrates most clearly the extent to which

Hannah took into her own hands the matter of her childlessness and asked the Lord for a son. She visited the shrine, made her request and underlined it with a vow, persisted in spite of Eli's lack of comprehension, and when the time came, kept her promise (1 Sam. 1.9-16, 24-28).

The three models illustrate Hannah's uniqueness and provide the hermeneutical lens through which this study analyzes the biblical and later versions of the Hannah story. I will briefly introduce each of the four below.

Early Methods of Biblical Interpretation

The period of formative Judaism and early Christianity was a time of dynamic interpretation of the Bible, to address the beliefs and concerns of the people in light of their foundational traditions and documents. The resulting interpretations are the product of a variety of approaches and techniques. This section discusses the typical characteristics and processes of early interpretation as well as elements particular to individual documents.

Beginning after the Babylonian exile, the early Jewish approach to biblical interpretation had five characteristics that expressed the developing concerns and beliefs of the community. These are free midrashic development, insertion of theological views, avoidance of anthropomorphic references to the Deity, respect for Israel and its elders, and use of contemporary geographical names for ancient places.[20] I will comment on the first four of these because they occur in the later versions of the Hannah story. These tendencies will be discussed in greater detail in chapters 3 and 4.

Free midrashic development involves additions to the story, ranging in length from single words to lengthy passages. The additions served to embellish the original text in order to edify, educate and entertain the audience, usually the congregation of a synagogue assembled for worship. The results were paraphrases and free retellings that incorporated the second, third and fourth interpretative characteristics.

Midrash expanded the biblical text with theological views important to the contemporary community. In the first century CE, belief in

20. M. McNamara, *Targum and Testament: Aramaic Paraphrases of the Hebrew Bible. A Light on the New Testament* (Grand Rapids: Eerdmans, 1972), pp. 31-34.

messianism and future life figured prominently among the communities who were disheartened and disillusioned by their conditions in the Roman Empire. Both of these teachings appear in *Biblical Antiquities* and *Targum of the Prophets*, and will be discussed in greater detail in the analyses of those materials.

In an effort to respect the commandment against graven images of God, interpreters described the Deity in concepts rather than the ancient anthropomorphisms found in the Bible. This tendency had already begun during the exile, and is evident when one contrasts the Yahwistic and Priestly writings in the Pentateuch. It continued under the influence of the Greek philosophical traditions. For example, *Targum of the Prophets* describes the divine defeats of Israel's enemies as 'the mighty works of God, who is powerful in the world' (*Targ. Neb.* 1 Sam. 2.6).

The later versions emphasize respect for Israel and its elders. First-century writings highlighted the leadership of the priests at a time when Roman authorities had removed virtually all political power from the Jews. This tendency is particularly evident in *Biblical Antiquities*, in the expanded role the text assigns to Eli.

While Luke's Infancy Narrative is not regarded as a Jewish work, it reflects literary characteristics typical of the Jewish writings familiar to its author and to all the early Jewish Christians. Their efforts to portray Christianity as distinct from Judaism are recorded in the patterns of thought and expression typical of the Jewish communities in which they lived. The occurrence in Luke's Infancy narrative of the four characteristics mentioned above will become evident in the discussion in ch. 5.

But along with these similarities, each later version contains distinctive characteristics as well. Each involves a different interpretive process, resulting in a different genre. The targumic version changes only the poetic text, and leaves the narrative intact. The changes add a large number of words and phrases to the original. The resulting apocalypse rehearses divine guidance throughout Israel's history and into the future. *Pseudo-Philo*'s account expands both poem and narrative, again adding some words and phrases and eliminating others. The resulting poem is a testament given at the point of transition from rule by judges, to rule by kings. The entire passage develops Hannah's status and role, as well as those of Eli. Luke's reconfiguration expands and rearranges the original, resulting in more complex poems and narrative. Thus each of the later interpretations evolved into a new entity with its own particular emphasis.[21] The specific processes and their results will become more evident throughout the following chapters.

21. J.E. Cook, 'Hannah's Later Songs: A Study in Comparative Methods of Interpretation', in C.A. Evans and J.A. Sanders (eds.), *Early Christian Interpretation of the Scriptures of Israel: Investigation and Proposals* (JSNTSup, 148; SSEJC, 5; Sheffield: Sheffield Academic Press, 1998), pp. 241-61.

Chapter 2

HANNAH IN 1 SAMUEL

The biblical story of Hannah forms the basis of the current study. In this chapter I review recent scholarly attention to the story in 1 Samuel and in its various larger contexts. These include textual, source, redaction and canonical questions as well as anthropological, literary and historical concerns about the narrative and the poem. Then I discuss the Hannah story's plot, analyze the Song, and relate the whole to the barren mother type. These aspects overlap with and give expression to the theological themes, particularly human and divine roles in the reform of the priesthood and institution of the monarchy.

Textual, Source and Redaction Issues

Recent Samuel scholarship nuances earlier information on textual questions, sources and redaction with the aid of computer-assisted research and the additional insights of anthropological, political and literary readings.[1]

Textual Studies

Textual studies illustrate the complex interrelationships among the ancient texts. For example, F.H. Polak's statistical analysis of the LXX, 4QSamᵃ, and MT versions concludes, '4QSamᵃ and the parent text of the Old Greek of the book of Samuel descend from one common exemplar (ב), which differs from the ancestor of MT and represents a revision of the ancient text'. R.P. Gordon cautions against an overly facile explanation of textual issues in Samuel based on haplography. And B.A. Taylor's two-volume study of the Lucianic Manuscripts in 1 Reigns concludes:

---

1. For a discussion of the textual issues in Samuel, see Cook, 'Text and Contexts', pp. 3-11.

It is necessary now for future research to take a fresh look at the relationships between the Lucianic (majority) text, the Hebrew texts, and the
Old Latin, the principal sources of the conclusion that the Lucianic text
is (essentially) the Old Greek. The analyses of these relationships must
begin from the premise that the Lucianic text in 1 Reigns is not the Old
Greek, and from there establish the nature of the interrelationships.[2]

A. Aejmelaeus studies the textual differences among the Greek texts,
and suggests that knowledge of the methods and characteristics of different translations can illuminate our understanding of their
differences.[3]

Source and Redaction Studies
Source and redaction studies show the complex external and internal
dynamics in the emergence of the Israelite monarchy. Within the
Deuteronomistic History the importance of the Samuel corpus lies in its
description and interpretation of the transition from the period of the
judges to the beginning of the monarchy. The era was characterized by
urban growth and its accompanying social stratification, conflict and
administrative shifts exacerbated externally by Philistine oppression.
The Philistine victories are explained as punishment for Israel's sin, but
opinions differ as to which sector of the population—the priests or the
people—were largely responsible for their defeat.

R.P. Gordon looks at the question of the historical backdrop to the
emergence of the monarchy and the narrative traditions associated with
Samuel of Ramah, to clarify the historicity of Samuel. He concludes
that internally, social stratification and conflict accompanied by an
increase in the population and the accompanying administrative needs
which were poorly handled by Samuel's sons played as significant a
part in the need for a new form of government as did the threat from the
Philistines. In his view, the tradition of Samuel as prophet, judge and

2.   B.A. Taylor, *The Lucianic Manuscripts of 1 Reigns*. II. *Analysis* (Atlanta:
Scholars Press, 1993), p. 128.
3.   A. Aejmelaeus, 'The Septuagint of 1 Samuel', in *idem*, (ed.) *On the Trail of
Septuagint Translators* (Kampen: Kok, 1993), pp. 131-49 (136); R.P. Gordon, 'The
Problem of Haplography in 1 and 2 Samuel', in G.J. Brooke and B. Lindars (eds.),
Septuagint, Scrolls and Cognate Writings (Atlanta: Scholars Press, 1992), pp. 131-
58; F.H. Polak, 'Statistics and Textual Filiation: The Case of 4QSam[a]/LXX (With a
note on the text of the Pentateuch)', in G.J. Brooke and B. Lindars (eds.), *Septuagint, Scrolls and Cognate Writings* (Atlanta: Scholars Press, 1992), pp. 215-76
(215).

kingmaker seems to come from prophetic circles and Deuteronomistic editors. But the boy's sleeping at the Shiloh shrine and his association with the high place of Ramah would not have come from a later time, and thus are probably historically accurate. Gordon concludes that Samuel might actually have participated in making Saul king. But he acknowledges a lack of consensus on this matter, citing others who say that later prophetic circles added that information in order to relate kingship with prophetic auspices. According to Gordon, Samuel the last judge figured prominently in the transition to the monarchy by presiding over the return of the Ark from the Philistines.[4]

Canonical Contexts

Recent canonical analyses of Samuel further the work of redaction studies by examining the book's place within the different versions of the canon. Whether one looks at the corpus in its Masoretic location or its place in the Septuagint influences what one finds. When 1 Samuel follows Judges in what has been called 'the extended book of Judges', Samuel is the last of the judges. 'So the Philistines were subdued' (1 Sam. 7.13) under Samuel repeats the formula found in Judg. 3.30; 4.23; 8.28; 11.33; marking the subduing of Moab, Jabin, Midian and the Ammonites. But when 1 Samuel follows Ruth a different configuration results. Both books read 'a certain man of…' in their first verse. And they recount the steps taken by Naomi and Hannah to protect their family lines.[5]

Similarly, whether one identifies the Samuel corpus as 1–2 Samuel, following Judges and preceding Kings, or as 1–2 Kingdoms, followed by 3–4 Kingdoms, nuances the way one reads it in relation to the monarchy. The first underscores its transitional aspect while the second links it more closely with the monarchy.[6]

4.   R.P. Gordon, 'Who Made the Kingmaker? Reflections on Samuel and the Institution of the Monarchy', in A.R. Millard, J.K. Hoffmeier and D.W. Baker (eds.), *Faith, Tradition, and History: Old Testament Historiography in its Near Eastern Context* (Winona Lake, IN: Eisenbrauns, 1994), pp. 255-69 (255-63); P.K. McCarter, Jr, 'The Books of Samuel', in S.L. McKenzie and M.P. Graham (eds.), *The History of Israel's Traditions: The Heritage of Martin Noth* (Sheffield: Sheffield Academic Press, 1994), pp. 260-80.

5.   D. Jobling, 'What, If Anything, Is 1 Samuel?', *SJOT* 7 (1993), pp. 17-31 (23).

6.   W.J. Dumbrell, 'The Content and Significance of the Books of Samuel:

Thus, reading Hannah within 'the extended book of Judges'

> maximizes her relative strength and independence. To read her in
> 'Samuel' downplays these aspects in favor of seeing her as involved in
> the transition to monarchy, and as herself exemplifying the status of
> women in monarchical Israel. To read her in '1 Samuel' is to confirm
> this separation between the world of Samuel and that of Judges, in as
> much as Ruth acts as a buffer between these worlds, and further val-
> orizes monarchy.[7]

But as part of the former prophets, the Samuel corpus highlights the
role of the prophets in establishing and maintaining the monarchy. For
instance, 1 Samuel 1–6 can be seen as preparing the way for the monarchy. Chapters 1–3 do this by introducing Samuel as the prophet who
would preside over its establishment, while chs. 4–6 focus on the Ark
as a manifestation of divine power and purpose among the people.
However, later redactors might have included the traditions about
Samuel the prophet, judge and kingmaker to help validate the monarchy as a divine institution.[8]

Another redactional question has to do with the relationship between
the narrative and poetic sections of the books. Until recently, the tendency was to assume that they were later additions to the Samuel
corpus. Opinions varied regarding the dates of composition and insertion of the poems.[9]

Their Place and Purpose Within the Former Prophets', *JETS* 33 (1990), pp. 49-62.

7.   Jobling, 'What, If Anything', pp. 29-30.

8.   A.F. Campbell, 'Past History and Present Text: The Clash of Classical and
Post-Critical Approaches to Biblical Text', *AusBR* 39 (1991), pp. 1-18 (9).

9.   Scholars who consider the Song a later addition pass quickly over it or omit
it altogether from their studies. For example, among the commentators
J. Mauchline, *1 and 2 Samuel* (NCB; London: Oliphants, 1971), omits it entirely
from his discussion of sources, pp. 16-17; H.P. Smith, *A Critical and Exegetical
Commentary on the Books of Samuel* (ICC; Edinburgh: T. & T. Clark, 1899), suggests only that it 'is now universally conceded to be an independent composition
inserted in the text from some poetical collection like our own book of Psalms', p.
xix; H.W. Hertzberg, *I & II Samuel: A Commentary* (OTL; Philadelphia: Westminster Press, 1964), also thinks that it was an already existing psalm inserted by
the compiler. He does, however, discuss the poem as a theological reflection on
Samuel's birth and life (p. 31); McCarter, Jr, proposes a careful reconstruction and
translation of the text that includes the Qumran materials. But he does not mention
the poem in his discussion of the book's literary history, *I Samuel*, pp. 12-30; and
several studies of early Hebrew poetry likewise omit the Song of Hannah from their
discussion. F.M. Cross and D.N. Freedman do not include it in their *Studies of*

Recent studies see the poems as integral to the narrative, not mere additions, regardless of their dates of insertion. The two main poems, the Song of Hannah in 1 Sam. 2.1-10 and David's Words in 2 Sam. 22.1–23.7, focus the reader's approach to 1–2 Samuel in several ways. They characterize human activity during that period in history. And they present YHWH in orthodox terms as an alternative to the unorthodox and problematic depictions of the Deity throughout the two books.[10]

Literary Readings: Backward and Forward in the Text
Canonical shape also influences the perspectives of various literary studies. For example, reading backward links 1 Samuel directly to Judges in MT and Ruth in LXX. And reading forward links Samuel with the journeys of the Ark from Shiloh to its eventual home in the Temple in Jerusalem and with the foundation of the monarchy.

More specifically, reading the Hannah narrative backward and forward situates her solidly in the traditions and history of Israel. A backward look links her with the barren women of Genesis and relates her Song to the Song of Deborah (Judg. 5) 'with its sweeping away of the vaunted power of kings by the waters of Kishon; and perhaps also to

Ancient Yahwistic Poetry (SBLDS, 21; Missoula, MT: Scholars Press, 1975). But D.N. Freedman does include it in his 'Divine Names and Titles in Early Hebrew Poetry', in *idem*, (ed.) *Pottery, Poetry, and Prophecy: Studies in Early Hebrew Poetry* (Winona Lake, IN: Eisenbrauns, 1980), pp. 77-129. D.A. Robertson, *Linguistic Evidence in Dating Early Hebrew Poetry* (SBLDS, 3; Missoula, MT: Printing Department, University of Montana, 1972), also omits the poem from his study. For a summary of findings regarding the dates of composition and insertion, see Cook, 'Text and Contexts', pp. 29-48.

10. The focus on human history is found, for example, in W. Brueggemann, 'I Samuel 1: A Sense of a Beginning', *ZAW* 102 (1990), pp. 33-48; B. Childs, *Introduction to the Old Testament as Scripture* (Philadelphia: Fortress Press, 1979), p. 273; F.O. García-Treto, '"A Mother's Paean, A Warrior's Dirge": Reflections on the Use of Poetic Inclusions in the Books of Samuel', *Shofar* 11 (1993), pp. 51-64 (55); V.P. Long, 'Scenic, Succinct, Subtle: An Introduction to the Literary Artistry of 1 & 2 Samuel', *Presbyterion* 19 (1993), pp. 32-47 (34); R. Polzin, *Samuel and the Deuteronomist: A Literary Study of the Deuteronomic History Part Two, I Samuel* (New York: Harper & Row, 1989), p. 31. Depictions of YHWH are found in J.S. Ackerman, 'Who Can Stand before YHWH, This Holy God? A Reading of 1 Samuel 1–15', *Prooftexts* 11 (1991), pp. 1-24 (6-7); R.C. Bailey, 'The Redemption of YHWH: A Literary Critical Function of the Songs of Hannah and David', *BibInt* 3 (1995), pp. 213-31 (217-20) .

the antimonarchical fable of Jotham—a man's song, but one which finds its fulfillment in a woman's assassination of a king' (Judg. 9.8-15, 53-55)! And a forward look highlights Hannah's contributions to priestly reform and the institution of the monarchy, and relates it to David's words in 2 Samuel 22.[11]

Reading the Song of Hannah backward and forward raises questions about its relation to the monarchy. In terms of time, a backward look suggests to Jobling that the poem does not look forward to the monarchy, but rather assumes its existence. If this is so, the final half-verse anachronistically supports the monarchy in a non-monarchical poem.[12]

Canonical-Literary Studies: Interaction Between Poetry and Prose
Additionally, for García-Treto, the poems of Hannah and David create a pause in the action, during which the reader is invited to savor the meaning of events, to become more acquainted with the character who speaks, and to reflect on the meaning of the passage in the context of the whole corpus. When considered together, the poems reveal the narrator's agenda, a 'political theology in which divine intervention in human affairs is a primal and determining force, albeit one whose revolutionary shifts of direction, overturning the mighty to establish the weak, are always difficult to predict'. The poems permit the exilic author to grieve over the loss of the kingdom, just as Hannah looked forward to its promise. The reversals that began and ended the monarchy are the stuff of the poetic reflections.[13]

Canonical and Theological Issues
Canonical studies often focus on theological content, particularly the divine role in the institution of the monarchy. To that end Brueggemann concludes that the Samuel corpus wishes to assert that the monarchy appeared because of the inscrutable, inexplicable initiative of YHWH. His analysis shows that a first reading appears to balance the causes of the monarchy as both divine and human. But a closer look reveals the divine centrality throughout.[14]

Dumbrell finds that the books of Samuel 'point to the underlying theological assumptions within which such a political concept as monarchy in Israel could gain point'. Within that frame of reference,

11. Polzin, *Samuel*, p. 26.
12. Jobling, 'What, If Anything', p. 28.
13. García-Treto, 'Paean', pp. 55-62.
14. Brueggemann, 'Sense of a Beginning', pp. 33-48.

Dumbrell identifies two levels of movement in the two books. The first, the movement of the Ark from Shiloh to Jerusalem, represents development from a stance of indifferent response to divine kingship to one of required response to divine kingship. Hannah's quiet piety contrasts with the corrupt priesthood at Shiloh followed by the end of 2 Samuel which foreshadows a permanent Temple in Jerusalem with David's purchase of the threshing floor.[15]

The second level of movement goes from despair to hope: Hannah's barrenness gives way to the prophetic word to Samuel in 1 Samuel 3. Eli and his family cause the coming destruction. But Hannah and her family enable the rebuilding of faith to occur. The Song of Hannah states the new directions to come in Israel's fortunes with the establishment of messianic kingship, which finally demonstrates divine kingship. And the Song anticipates divine reversals of the directions set by Israel. This view highlights the relationship between divine and human interaction in the development of kingship.[16]

Ackerman wrestles with the interplay between God and humans in 1 Samuel 1–15. He sees in the narrative a search for a leader who is able to stand before God on the people's behalf. He concludes that no one can do it but someone must, in view of 'the holiness and mystery of God, which renders that quest problematic'.[17]

Bailey focuses on the contrasts between the portrayals of God in the narrative in 1–2 Samuel and in the poems. He sees the ambiguous and uncertain divine action and inaction as a description of Israel's experience of the Exile. And he concludes, 'The final form of the book proclaims to the exiles, "While your experience of God may be as capricious as the events of this book, your hope, however, must be grounded in the God of these Songs of Hannah and David"'.[18]

These recent approaches open up the possibility of what D. Jobling identifies as two different interpretations of the narrative, including God's action and Hannah's initiative. One might say that Hannah acted for her own reasons, and God continued her actions for reasons beyond her imagining. Or one could say that Hannah knew what she was doing, and was therefore 'responsible for the consequences of her initiative'.[19]

---

15. Dumbrell, 'Content and Significance', pp. 49-62.

16. Dumbrell, 'Content and Significance', pp. 49-51.

17. Ackerman, 'Who Can Stand', p. 1.

18. Bailey, 'Redemption', p. 231.

19. D. Jobling, 'Hannah's Desire', in D.W. Cotter (ed.), *1 Samuel* (Berit Olam;

My study assumes from the foregoing analysis of canonical issues that both interpretations coexist in the final form of the story. A look at the contours of that story lays the foundation on which to develop this claim.

The Hannah Story in 1 Samuel

The story of Hannah opens 1 Samuel and continues from 1.1 to 2.21, intercalated by the story of Eli's corrupt sons in 2.12-17. The Hannah narrative develops in two movements: the first, 'Hannah Finds her Voice' and the second, 'Hannah Uses her Voice'. Each movement has three parts. The first begins with an introductory statement about Elkanah's family (vv. 1-2), followed by a record of Elkanah's annual trips to Shiloh (vv. 3-18). It includes Hannah's vow, which she made during her decisive visit to the shrine (vv. 9-18). Her vow announces her determination in spite of Peninnah's taunts and Elkanah's lack of understanding, and in spite of Eli's inability to see. The first movement concludes with the mention of their return home (v. 19a).[20] The second movement develops in a parallel pattern. It begins with a statement about Hannah's family, announcing the birth and naming of Samuel (vv. 19b-20), followed by a description of his first years (1.21–2.10). It includes Hannah's climactic fulfillment of her vow at the Shiloh shrine, during which she sang her Song (1.24–2.10). The second movement concludes with the record of Elkanah's return home. After the intercalation the narrative concludes with a brief mention of Hannah's continuing care for her son in 2.18-21.

A closer look at each part illustrates how the story develops and expresses the various tensions between divine and human initiative. In the first movement, part one, the introductory statement gives geographical and biographical information about Elkanah's family. It names four generations of his ancestors of the tribe of Ephraim, and situates his home in that territory, in the town of Ramathaim.[21] Then it

Collegeville, MN: Liturgical Press, 1998), pp. 131-42 (136).

20. It is puzzling that the narrative reports that only Elkanah returned home, even though Hannah surely went, too (1 Sam. 2.11).

21. C. Meyers locates the town at the site of modern Rentis based on linguistic and environmental analysis, in 'An Ethnoarchaeological Analysis of Hannah's Sacrifice', in D.P. Wright, D.N. Freedman and A. Hurvitz (eds.), *Pomegranates and Golden Bells: Studies in Biblical, Jewish, and Near Eastern Ritual, Law, and*

names his two wives, indicating that Peninnah had children but Hannah did not (1.1-2). That brief bit of information alludes to significant tension and foreshadows its influence on the life of the family.

The second part draws the reader's attention to time and place: the annual offering of first-fruits of the land to the Lord at the Shiloh shrine, where the Ark was kept at that time and where Eli's sons Hophni and Phinehas served as priests. Their introduction into the narrative at this point foreshadows the more explicit account of how they abused their office and the people they served. That information appears after the family's return from dedicating Samuel (2.12-17). But the earlier mention of the sons' names raises the clear possibility that Hannah and Elkanah had first-hand experience of the priests' violations of their office.[22]

The tension develops in this part as the consequences of Hannah's childlessness, Peninnah's jealousy and Elkanah's lack of understanding are made known. But these dynamics develop in an unexpected way because Hannah does not respond to the problematic words of her co-wife or husband.

Various interpretations have been offered to explain the miscommunication among the family members, from 'arrogant egotism' on Elkanah's part to his preoccupation with his own concerns to his presumption that he is enough for his wife. Regardless of the precise interpretation one makes of Elkanah's words, he does not appear to be preoccupied about Hannah providing him with offspring.[23]

Literature in Honor of Jacob Milgrom (Winona Lake, IN: Eisenbrauns, 1995), pp. 77-91 (85-86) .

22. Jobling, 'Hannah's Desire', pp. 134-35.

23. Y. Amit's conclusion that Elkanah's questions exemplify his arrogant egotism seems a bit strong for two reasons. First, they might simply illustrate the miscommunication that can occur between people, particularly of different genders, when speaking of important concerns. And second, it makes Hannah very male-dependent by suggesting that she suffered from Elkanah's insensitivity but not from Peninnah's obnoxiousness. See '"Am I Not More Devoted To You Than Ten Sons?" (1 Samuel 1.8): Male and Female Interpretations', in A. Brenner (ed.), *A Feminist Companion to Samuel and Kings* (Sheffield: Sheffield Academic Press, 1994), pp. 68-76 (75). L.R. Klein discusses Elkanah's preoccupation in 'Hannah: Marginalized Victim and Social Redeemer', in A. Brenner, (ed.), *A Feminist Companion to Samuel and Kings* (Sheffield: Sheffield Academic Press, 1994), pp. 77-92 (87-89). C. Ozick relates Elkanah's questions to the status of humans in the likeness of the Creator in 'Hannah and Elkanah: Torah as the Matrix for Feminism', in

Her family members' lack of understanding sets the stage for the third part. It describes Hannah's decisive visit to the shrine, where she asked for a son and vowed to dedicate him to the Lord. These actions had several conflicting implications: she looked outside her family for the support lacking within it; she took a step to achieve her social role as wife and protect her family line. But in vowing to dedicate the child to the Lord she also gave up the normal familial relationship between mother and son, thus increasing the tension in the narrative. In fact, Hannah's promise unites her purpose with that of her husband: she promises to give God her own first-fruits, like Elkanah. And her promise determines her own future as well as that of Israel. Her action marks a change in her, toward a determination and decisiveness that become her hallmark characteristics.

At the shrine Hannah encounters another uncomprehending person, the priest Eli. This time she does not remain silent, but responds to her interlocutor, telling him his error in thinking she was drunk, but giving very little information about herself. After his uncomprehending blessing the narrative reports Hannah's transformation by observing that she ate and drank with Elkanah and that her face was no longer sad.

The narrative does not specify precisely what caused the change that came over Hannah. It leaves open the possibility that perhaps her vow, or Eli's blessing, or her meal with Elkanah made the difference. Or maybe her new demeanor results from her victory over Eli's wicked sons: the child she will return to God will serve as a worthy priest, taking the place of Hophni and Phinehas, so those who visit the shrine will no longer be subjected to harassment and abuse.

With that the first movement ends, and a brief transitional and biographical note introduces the second movement. Verses 19-20 recount that after a final visit to the shrine the family returned home and Elkanah 'knew' Hannah. The reader is assured that Hannah's prayer will be answered and her promise kept in the report that the Lord remembered her and she bore a son, naming him Samuel in honor of her request. These events, narrated in a straightforward style, highlight the importance of human actions in the story. For example, the reference to

C. Buchmann and C. Spiegel (eds.), *Out of the Garden: Women Writers on the Bible* (New York: Fawcett Columbine, 1994), pp. 88-93 (90-91). M. Falk interprets Elkanah's questions as his missing the point in 'Reflections on Hannah's Prayer', in C. Buchmann and C. Spiegel (eds.), *Out of the Garden: Women Writers on the Bible* (New York: Fawcett Columbine, 1994), pp. 94-102 (97).

Elkanah and Hannah's intercourse is unique among the barren mother stories. That information appears in other birth stories, for example Adam and Eve (Gen. 4) and Cain and his wife (4.17), but not in any barren mother accounts other than the Hannah narrative. And divine remembering follows human action: Hannah's initiative resulted in the Lord's gift of a son.

In keeping with the highly nuanced situation in which Hannah now finds herself, she names her son and associates his name with her request at Shiloh.

Then in the second part of the narrative, in which the family continues its tradition of annual trips to Shiloh, Hannah decides to stay home and care for her son.[24] Elkanah accedes to her resolution.

The climax of the second movement parallels that of the first. After Hannah weaned Samuel she took him to Shiloh in fulfillment of her vow. On her arrival she greeted Eli with a reference to her earlier visit and announced the terms of her vow and its fulfillment. With that she sang in praise of the God who overturns the situations of all people. (I will discuss the Song in detail later in the chapter.) Anthropological studies clarify the ancient customs to which the text alludes.[25]

Meyers demonstrates that materials for sacrifice are integrally related to socioeconomic conditions. The three elements of Hannah's sacrifice are local and individualistic, such as are rooted in an agrarian, village-centered tribal economy. Particularly noteworthy is the absence of olive oil among her gifts. This information helps to locate Hannah's village at the site of modern Rentis, an area where the subsistence regime

24. The Syriac reinforces Hannah's decisiveness and the Lord's blessing of it with the variant reading, 'May the Lord establish that which goes out of your mouth' (1.23).

25. The narrative is ambiguous regarding who actually went to Shiloh. 1 Sam. 1.24 indicates that Hannah took Samuel along with the votive offerings. Verse 25 states that they slew the bull and they brought the child to Eli. The only possible antecedent for 'they' is Hannah and Elkanah, assuming that 'they' refers to the same people both times it appears. Then vv. 28b and 2.11 vary in the different versions regarding who worshiped at Shiloh ('he', 'they') and who went home afterward ('Elkanah', 'they'). My study relies on the transitional 2.1a, which specifies that Hannah prayed the Song; and it assumes from the flow of the narrative, especially 2.19, that Hannah returned home with Elkanah afterward. For a general discussion of the variant readings see Cook, 'Text and Contexts', pp. 61-63. For specific comments about the verses in question, see McCarter, Jr, *I Samuel*, pp. 56-58, 78; and Walters, 'Hannah and Anna', pp. 398-403.

matches the elements of her sacrifice. In addition, the materials for sacrifice indicate that the ceremony took place at a time prior to the establishment of a pan-Israelite religion because the elements do not correspond to those specified for official religious practice.[26]

Meyers supports her thesis by situating Hannah's sacrifice in the context of family religion, as it existed prior to the structuring of pilgrimage festivals prescribed in the Pentateuchal legal texts. Family religion at the time probably gave men and women virtually the same roles, except for priestly eligibility which was reserved for men. The textual question that arises with regard to 1 Sam. 1.24, around the issue of who brought the sacrifice to Shiloh, can be enlightened in a way congruent with Hannah's prominence in the narrative, and with what we can infer about female participation in cultic events prior to the monarchy and concomitant establishment of pan-Israelite religion. Numbers 30.6-8 makes a woman's vow subject to her husband's veto. That law may be later than the activities recorded in 1 Samuel 1. Women in early Israel probably did make and carry out their own vows. Ethnographic research identifies pilgrimages and concomitant votive acts as two of the most characteristic religious acts of women. And the text makes no suggestion that Elkanah made any judgment about Hannah's vow.[27]

Meyers further explains that women's public roles and social influence were frequently more significant during times of social upheaval and political decentralization with no dominant national power structure. 'It is just at such unsettled times that all persons with marginal access to power find themselves able to transcend the normal criteria that might otherwise limit their actions.' For example, Hannah's sacrifice bridges the personal and public spheres. Her motive is purely individual and personal. But her visit to the Shiloh shrine where she interacts with the leading priestly figure of the day (Eli) and her behavior foreshadow her son's national significance. As such, the narrative is much more than a story of family life; it moves into the realm of national service.[28]

---

26. Meyers, 'Ethnoarchaeological Analysis', pp. 77-91.

27. C. Meyers, 'The Hannah Narrative in Feminist Perspective', in J. Coleson and V. Matthews (eds.), *Go To the Land I Will Show You* (Winona Lake, IN: Eisenbrauns, 1996), pp. 117-26 (122-25).

28. Meyers, 'Hannah Narrative', p. 126.

The account then notes that Elkanah returned home. One might wonder if Hannah stayed with her son at Shiloh. After all, fulfilling her vow necessitated leaving him with the priest who lacked insight. She might well have wondered how safe Samuel would be in the care of such a man.

But after the intercalated story of Eli's corrupt sons (further reason for Hannah to wonder about her own son's safety) the narrative implies that Hannah lived in Ramah with Elkanah when the conclusion explains that they made the annual trip together, and each year she took him a little robe. She did not completely relinquish care of him, but continued to look after his well-being. And we can be sure she took the opportunity to make certain that her son was receiving proper care from his mentor at the shrine. Eli blessed the couple, praying that they would have other children, after which Hannah had three more sons and two daughters.[29]

The Song of Hannah

The biblical Song of Hannah is a hymn sung by Hannah at the Shiloh shrine on the occasion of her dedication of her son Samuel to the Lord. She had promised to give back the son she requested from the Lord to remove her barrenness. The words of the hymn do not directly address her particular situation, but rather praise the God who reverses the fortunes of all, upsets the status quo, and offers particular protection to the more vulnerable members of society. Hannah sings a carefully crafted hymn that expresses the specific concerns of an agricultural and pastoral society in the Galilean hills: the enemies are hunger, barrenness and poverty. Likewise it expresses the conviction that those who rely on the Deity will be protected and rewarded with reversals of fortune in their daily life.[30]

The believing community in late eighth- and seventh-century Judah wrestled with the issue of trust in divine dominion in the face of Assyrian expansion. During that time the Song of Hannah and the

29. Brueggemann's schema reaches a different conclusion: that God's action prevails throughout. He reaches this conclusion by using four 'Yahwistic' statements as the organizing pillars of his schema in 'Sense of a Beginning', p. 33.

30. For a detailed discussion of the genre of the Song, see Cook, 'Text and Contexts', pp. 87-101.

Samuel corpus served to bolster the people's conviction that the monarchy was a divinely sanctioned institution. And the people were urged to depend on the divine king to protect them from military and political threats by Assyria and from the various maneuvers of the smaller powers who tried to resist the Assyrian onslaught.[31]

It can be outlined in the following way. After the transitional v. 1a the Song divides easily into three hymnic parts: introduction (vv. 1b-e), body (vv. 2a-10d) and conclusion (v. 10e). The body of the Song contains five stanzas which praise divine attributes (vv. 2-3), guidance (vv. 4-5) and deeds (vv. 6a-8b); explain the goal and rationale for the Deity's actions (vv. 8c-9c); and praise a second set of divine deeds (v. 10a-d). The final stich (v. 10e) concludes the poem. The Song appears below according to this division, with each stich numbered according to verse. The stanzas are numbered for easy reference.

Stanza 1: Transition	1a	Then Hannah, praying,[32] said,
Stanza 2: Introduction	b	'My heart delights in YHWH;
	c	my horn triumphs in my God.[33]
	d	My mouth gloats over my enemies;[34]
	e	indeed, I jubilate at your deliverance.[35]
Stanza 3: YHWH's Attributes	2a	There is no one holy like YHWH
	b	and there is no rock[36] like our God.[37]

---

31. For details about the provenance of the Song, see Cook, 'Text and Contexts', pp. 45-60.

32. This reading appears in MT, LXX[L] and LXX[B]. Its presence in the text parallels the formulaic introductions to prayers in 2 Sam. 1.17-18 and 22.1-2 and Jon. 2.2.

33. With LXX, against MT and 4QSam[a], which repeats ביהוה.

34. The verbs in stichs b and e (שמח, עלץ) appear elsewhere as pairs in Pss. 5.12; 9.3; 68.4. There as well as here they celebrate the humble joy of those who praise the divine strength; L. Eslinger, *Kingship of God in Crisis: A Close Reading of 1 Samuel 1–12* (Bible and Literature Series; Sheffield: Almond Press, 1985), p. 103.

35. The stich agrees with MT.

36. With MT and 4QSam[a]. See J. Wellhausen, *Der Text der Bücher Samuelis* (Göttingen: Vandenhoeck & Ruprecht, 1871), p. 43; McCarter, Jr, *I Samuel*, p. 68; Smith, *Commentary*, p. 15; H.J. Stoebe, *Das Erste Buch Samuelis* (KAT, 8.1; Güterloh: Gerd Mohn, 1973), p. 101.

37. Against the versions, which insert an additional clause, כי אין בלתך, but each version inserts it in a different place in the stich. I omit the clause because the

3a Don't assert repeatedly 'Loftiness, loftiness';[38]

  b Don't let arrogance flow from your mouth.

  c For a God of knowledge is YHWH

  d and a God[39] who balances deeds.[40]

Stanza 4: YHWH's Guidance

4a The bows of the mighty are shattered,[41]

  b but the faltering equip themselves with strength.

5a The well-fed hire themselves out for bread,

  b but the hungry cease while[42]

  c the barren woman bears seven

  d and the one rich in sons languishes.

Stanza 5: YHWH's Deeds

6a It is YHWH who puts to death and restores to life,

  b who banishes to Sheol and raises up.

7a It is YHWH who impoverishes and makes wealthy,

  b who humbles and even[43] exalts.

8a Who raises from the dust the poor,

  b and from the garbage-heap lifts up the needy

variety of locations suggests a later addition. Wellhausen, *Text*, p. 43; S.R. Driver, *Notes on the Hebrew Text and the Topography of the Books of Samuel* (Oxford: Clarendon Press, 2nd edn, 1960), p. 24; McCarter, Jr, *I Samuel*, p. 69; Stoebe, *Erste Buch Samuelis*, p. 100; M. Weinfeld, *Deuteronomy and the Deuteronomic School* (Oxford: Oxford University Press, 1972), p. 49 n. 79; J. Weingreen, *Introduction to the Critical Study of the Text of the Hebrew Bible* (Oxford: Clarendon Press, 1982), pp. 86-87.

   38. With MT.

   39. With LXX in preference to MT *ketib* ולא and *qere* ולו.

   40. Following LXX. MT reads נתכנו. The passive verb form seems uncharacteristically weak compared to the other verbs in the Song; McCarter, Jr, *I Samuel*, p. 69.

   41. MT has singular subject and plural verb.

   42. With MT. For a detailed discussion of the textual complexities of the stich, see Cook, 'Text and Contexts', pp. 77-79.

   43. Following Driver's identification of the poetic use of אף as emphatic introduction of a new thought in *Notes*, p. 26. See also BDB, p. 64; R.J. Williams, *Hebrew Syntax: An Outline* (Toronto: University of Toronto Press, 2nd edn, 1976), p. 64, par. 384.

Stanza 6: YHWH's Goal and Rationale	c	To seat (them) with nobles
	d	and bequeath to them a throne of honor.
	e	For YHWH's are the pillars of the earth;
	f	(he) sets upon them the world[44]
	9a	And supports the feet of his faithful,
	b	but the wicked are silenced in the darkness.[45]
	c	For not by strength is one strong.
Stanza 7: YHWH's Deeds	10a	YHWH shatters his adversary,
	b	the Most High thunders from heaven.[46]
	c	YHWH judges the ends of the earth
	d	and bestows strength on his king;
Stanza 8: Conclusion	e	Let him exalt the horn of his anointed one.'

The arrangement highlights the Song's progression of ideas around the climactic sixth stanza in several ways.[47] The thought of the preceding stanzas progresses and intensifies from attributes to guidance to deeds, then to the divine goal and rationale. Then the second list of divine deeds creates an envelope with stanza 5 around the climactic goal statement. Stanza 6 is also the longest of the stanzas, highlighting divine intervention in human events by the creator and source of all creatures' strength.

Artistic Features of the Poem
In this section I will discuss the artistic features that unify the poem and convey its meaning. These include the various repetitive features such as word repetition, parallelisms, framing words, chiasms, repetition of sounds, as well as other features such as contrasts, synecdoches,

---

44. With MT.

45. Stichs 8e-9b are missing from LXX, which reads instead, 'He gives to the vower his vow, and blesses the year of the righteous', a line which is missing entirely from MT, and which is v. 9b in McCarter's reconstruction of 4QSam[a]. The diversity of readings of the verse is discussed in Cook, 'Text and Contexts', pp. 80-83.

46. Refer to Cook, 'Text and Contexts', pp. 84-85, for the textual complexities of stichs 10a and 10b and additions found in the versions.

47. For a detailed analysis of the textual, grammatical and rhetorical aspects of the poem, see Cook, 'Text and Contexts', pp. 61-86, 102-31.

merisms and biblical allusions. I will comment on their appearance and interplay to convey the meaning of the poem. In this analysis I will refer to the listener and the reader interchangeably, assuming that the Song originally was sung and also that current readers will read it aloud in order to appreciate the oral aspects of the poem.

The transitional stich announces to the reader the shift from prose words spoken to Eli (1.26-28a) and descriptive narrative (v. 28b) to poetic words to God, setting the liturgical tone of the prayer that follows. The stanza leads directly into Hannah's introductory statement of praise and jubilation.

In stanza 2 the intensity builds from one stich to the next, until in stich e the synecdoches 'heart' and 'mouth' (vv. 1b and d) give way to the subject 'I' (v. 1e) and Hannah addresses God directly for the only time in the poem. The synecdoches form an envelope around the word 'horn' (v. 1c). R. Polzin suggests that Hannah's enemies are those who oppose the establishment of the monarchy, while the poor and downtrodden are the kings of Israel, who will assume international stature.[48]

This leads into the body of the hymn, which begins with a six-stich stanza describing YHWH's attributes. The stanza is arranged in three pairs of stichs. The first and third pairs (vv. 2ab and 3cd) name the qualities of the Deity and form an envelope around the middle pair (v. 3ab), an aside to the haughty ones. The same two divine appelatives appear in v. 2ab as appeared in the introduction (v. 1bc), linking this stanza with the introduction.

The Song then goes on to describe the current situation under the guidance of the God who balances deeds. Here it contrasts not God and the haughty ones but people who customarily count on their own resources and those who have no personal assets on which to rely.

Contextually it contrasts the situations of the poor and the rich on the basis of their need to work. The normal arrangement has been upset; it is now not the poor who must earn their food, but those who are accustomed to having an abundance. A series of three stich pairs expresses the contrasting circumstances of the mighty, the wealthy, and the fertile and their opposites, the weak, the poor, and the barren.

As a result of divine guidance (stanza 4) the bows of the mighty are shattered,[49] the well-fed work for bread, the barren woman bears seven

---

48. Polzin, *Samuel*, p. 33.

49. The image of the shattered bow, which appears also in Jer. 51.56, suggests the insufficiency of human strength, a theme that comes to the fore in stich 9c;

(see also Ps. 113.9) while the faltering equip themselves with strength, the hungry rest and the woman with many children languishes. (The more concrete first stichs in the pairs reverse the pattern in the previous stanza with its more concrete second stichs.)

The reference to the barren woman is the only direct link between Hannah's Song and her particular situation. Even though the narrative context of the Song does not call Hannah עקרה (barren) it does state, 'The Lord had closed her womb' (1 Sam. 1.5). The allusion deepens the reader's appreciation of Hannah's former distress and present jubilation by recalling the stories of other women who shared her circumstances (Sarah, Rebekah, Rachel, Manoah's wife, the Shunammite woman and the woman in Ezra's vision, all of whom bore special sons through divine intervention). It highlights the Lord's ongoing protection of the vulnerable: the divine gift of offspring reminded the people of God's intervention in their lives.

In stanzas 5 and 7 (vv. 6a-8b, 10a-d) the Song enumerates the specific divine deeds that reverse fortunes, interpolated by an explanation of the goal and rationale for the divine action in stanza 6 (vv. 8c-9c). This chiastic arrangement underscores the purposefulness of God's actions on the people's behalf.

Stanza 5 contains the first list of divine deeds. In this stanza the ideas build one upon the other in a panoply of contrasting divine actions toward those in opposite circumstances: the self-sufficient and the vulnerable. In the first two pairs the contrasting verbs describe the extent of divine involvement. The parallelisms in the first pair (v. 6ab) contrast 'puts to death' and 'banishes to Sheol' with 'restores to life' and 'raises up'. And the contrasts form a merism: divine activity encompasses all of life from putting to death to restoring to life.

The climactic stanza 6, the longest and most irregular in the poem, states the goal toward which all the divine attributes, guidance and deeds strive (v. 8cd), and the rationale that impels the Deity toward that goal (vv. 8e-9c). The goal statement names the place of exaltation, the throne where God seats those who have been rescued from poverty. The next part of the stanza gives the rationale for the goal. It highlights the Deity's dominion over all creation, using imagery from ancient Near Eastern cosmology, as the reason for exalting the lowly. The rationale is further developed in the three stichs that follow.

Eslinger, *Kingship*, p. 109. The same verb appears in conjugated form in stich 10a, emphasizing divine strength that prevails over God's enemies.

The tristich highlights the contrasts in the rationale statement: vv. 8f and 9a focus on divine support of the world and its faithful, and v. 9b describes the opposite fate of the wicked.

The ideas progress in gradual steps: v. 8f describes the process of creation of the earth implicit in v. 8e; v. 9ab refers to the people on the earth (the faithful and the wicked). The images that connect vv. 8f and 9a highlight the motif of support: just as YHWH's pillars support the world, YHWH upholds the faithful. The synecdoche names 'feet' as the object of YHWH's support, continuing and developing the imagery: feet touch the ground. Divine support of human feet allows the faithful to stand on earth just as earth stands on its pillars, and also permits them to walk, with YHWH guiding them on their way. The imagery shifts in v. 9b, which describes the fate of the wicked. They live in darkness, in other words outside the safety of the created order. And they are silenced: they cannot thrive because they lack support.

Then v. 9c concludes from the experience of the wicked that strength, that is self-sufficiency, does not grant success. This climactic observation appears throughout the poem in the warning against arrogance and the descriptions of divine guidance and deeds reversing fortunes. Now the Song declares it in summary of the divine rationale.[50]

Having summarized the goal and rationale statement with a reminder of the limits of human strength (v. 9c), the Song moves to stanza 7, the second catalogue of divine deeds. The stanza develops the theme of divine power introduced in the previous stich.

This second list of divine deeds recalls the first by its use of יהוה (YHWH) to open the first and third stichs (v. 10a and c; see vv. 6a and 7a). The usage links the two lists and calls immediate attention to the divine performer of the actions. This contrasts sharply to the limitations of human strength, which the previous verse (9c) announced.

When the poem declares, 'He gives strength to his king', (v. 10d) it has already defined 'strength' variously as military force (v. 10a), the power of a storm (v. 10b) and the authority of a judge (v. 10c). And v. 10e repeats the verb רום from vv. 1c, 7b and 8b, enveloping the poem in the motif of divine strength. In v. 10b the similar-sounding ירעם alludes to the Sinai theophany, which occurred in the midst of a

---

50. This idea occurs frequently throughout the Hebrew Bible, for example, in Pss. 20.7-8; 44.4-8; and in Paul's writing in the New Testament, for example, in 2 Cor. 12.9-10.

thunderstorm (see Exod. 19.16-20).[51] Heaven, the place of thunder, pairs with 'earth' in v. 10c: the merism emphasizes again the universality of divine dominion, and the repetition of 'earth' from v. 8e strengthens the link between divine deeds and goal. And the motif of God judging the ends of the earth repeats the connotation of the God who balances deeds (v. 3d).

This very direct, straightforward structure duplicates that of stanza 2. Strong verbs appear in both stanzas. The subjects highlight the singer's praise and the Deity's power, unifying the beginning and end of the Song.

Stanza 8, the poem's conclusion, requests honor for the anointed one, alluding to the previous stanza ('king') and creating an envelope with v. 1c in its reference to the horn. Here, God is asked to exalt the anointed one's horn, attributing the action to the Deity as opposed to Hannah's action in v. 1c. These references serve to link the poem's end with its beginning, bringing the thought full circle and highlighting yet again divine deeds. But in fact, the poem ends abruptly after its several catalogues of divine activity: other than the shift in verb forms from v. 10b and the mention of the anointed one, the final stich seems to continue the list of deeds rather than to close the Song.

The foregoing analysis illustrates the abundance of formal and rhetorical features and their functions in the poem. But the individual segments have value not only in isolation; together they contribute to the overall artistry that conveys the meaning of the Song as a whole. This synthesis demonstrates how the different features contribute to the poem's primary theme of divine intervention and reversal of fortunes on behalf of the vulnerable.

The poem highlights several key stichs—'Indeed I jubilate at your deliverance' (v. 1e), 'For a God of knowledge is YHWH' (v. 3c), 'To seat them with nobles and bequeath to them a throne of honor, For YHWH's are the pillars of the earth' (v. 8cde), 'For not by strength does one succeed' (v. 9c)—by its use of various formal and rhetorical features that support and highlight them. For instance, the anacrusic elements that introduce each of them alert the reader to the major idea that follows. In addition, the interweaving patterns of pairs and chiasms emphasize the themes of the stichs. The pair in v. 8cd illustrates this

51. H.G. Perelmuter, 'Once a Pun a Preacher', in D. Bergant and J.T. Pawlikowski (eds.), *Harvest of a Dialogue* (New York: Ktav, 1997), pp. 74-91.

point: the chiastic verbal pattern begins and ends the two stichs in which the second, 'and bequeath to them a throne of honor', concretizes the first, 'to seat them with nobles'.

Chiastic features likewise underline the theme of contrast throughout the poem. In vv. 8f-9b, the two stichs have exactly reversed structures that support their opposite meanings, the downfall of the self-sufficient who ignore divine sovereignty contrasts with the divine support of the faithful.

The repeated use of רום (rise) highlights the motif of lifting up, three times to describe divine activity (vv. 7b, 8b, 10e) and once to specify the singer's jubilation (v. 1c). Two of these form the frame קרן (horn, vv. 1c and 10e), which unifies the Song around the tone and theme of exultation.

From the start the poem emphasizes that the divine actions on behalf of the vulnerable give rise to the poet's praise. Such deeds are possible on the part of a God of power; various images and metaphors describe the dimensions of divine strength and give a tone of immediacy to the entire poem.

The images frequently suggest physical strength; for example, 'rock', 'shattered bow', 'sets the world on its pillars', 'shatters the adversary', 'thunders from heaven'. Several imply intellectual power, such as 'God of knowledge who balances deeds', 'judges the ends of the earth', and 'bestows strength on his king'. This power serves the cause of justice: 'The bows of the mighty are shattered but the faltering equip themselves with strength; the well-fed hire themselves out for bread but the hungry cease, while the barren woman bears seven but the one rich in sons languishes' (vv. 4-5). Likewise, YHWH raises the poor from the dust and lifts up from the garbage-heap the needy, and supports the feet of the faithful while 'the wicked are silenced in the darkness'.

Finally, divine strength empowers others: the singer jubilates at divine deliverance; YHWH supports the feet of the faithful, bestows strength on the king and exalts the horn of the anointed. The incremental effect of these images and metaphors highlights the infinite power of the God to whom the poet sings, graphically demonstrating the reason for the Song's praise and the cause of the singer's celebration.

This consideration of the poem's formal and rhetorical features illustrates how they convey the rich meaning of the Song. The hymnic outline structures the Song for praise-giving. It announces the speaker's jubilation, describes divine attributes, guidance and deeds (the reasons for the singer's praise), and requests a divine blessing. The stanzas in the body build toward the climactic statement of the divine goal and rationale in stanza 6. Rhetorical features such as pairs, formulas, lists, chiasms, imagery and sound patterns highlight the key words and stichs and serve to unify the entire poem and enhance its oral, cultic character. The whole, a masterful hymn, praises YHWH who intervenes in the lives of the people and reverses fortunes of both the faithful and the self-sufficient.

The Song interacts in several ways with its narrative and historical contexts. It appears within the narrative of the birth of Samuel, the transitional event that set in motion the foundation of the Israelite monarchy. Hannah's barrenness links her with Sarah and all the 'barren mothers' of Israel through whom the divine promise of offspring was carried forward. The setting of the Song maintains the cultic tie to the Ark of the Covenant, which was housed at the time in the Shiloh shrine where Hannah prayed. And in the historical context of the Deuteronomistic History, the Song proclaims divine concern for people in exile whose experience would have them call it into question.

The Song's thanksgiving dimension arises from its place in the Hannah narrative, the most immediate context of the poem. She sings in gratitude for the gift of her son Samuel, at the moment when she in turn gives him back to God.

Unique Features of the Hannah Narrative

Chapter 1 demonstrated that Hannah's story follows the type of the barren mother in all three of its models. In fact, she is the only barren mother who can be seen in relation to all three. While Sarah and Rachel each fit two of the three, the others fit only one. This connection with all three models occurs partly because the Hannah story offers more details about Hannah, and partly because Hannah takes a more active role in the narrative than do the other women. But not only does the Hannah narrative follow the three models; it also contains unique elements that become clear in relation to each of them.

Barren Mother Models

In relation to the competition model, Hannah was unique in not becoming embroiled in competition. Peninnah tormented her, and in fact her torments brought Hannah's sadness to Elkanah's attention. But Hannah did not compete with her rival wife. In addition, both Elkanah and Eli tormented her. In Elkanah's case, it was in a complex effort to console her,[52] but in fact as a result she took the situation squarely into her own hands, went to the shrine, and spoke to the Lord, the only one who did not misunderstand her. Eli, too, tormented her from his lack of sight and insight in the exercise of his priestly stewardship at the shrine. But by then Hannah had found her voice, and was not intimidated or put off by Eli's cruel misunderstanding of her plight.

Like the other barren mothers Hannah bore a son through divine intervention, but the narrative also indicates that 'Elkanah knew his wife Hannah, and the Lord remembered her' (1 Sam. 1.19), the only time in all the barren mother narratives that human sexual intercourse is mentioned. In this way the text highlights both human and divine action, holding them in tension more strongly in this story than in the others.

Regarding the promise model, Hannah reversed the promise element: she herself rather than someone else made the promise. What is more, she formally and publicly made a vow to return her son to the Lord while speaking in the public shrine at Shiloh. It might be mentioned at this point that Hannah promised to give her son to the Lord. The tradition that he would be a nazirite most likely developed later, as 'one more case of the tendency to have various distinguished features and prominent offices converge in Samuel'.[53]

And the doubts expressed in the promise model were not Hannah's but Eli's: he accused her of public drunkenness. And in response Hannah offered a form of reassurance to him in her honest but non-committal response, which prompted Eli to bestow a generic blessing on her.

A similar observation can be made with regard to the request model. That is, Hannah made the request directly to God, not to another human being. And no one else made it on her behalf. What is more, she formalized it by making it in the Shiloh shrine, with a vow to return the desired son to the Lord. In fact, her visit to the shrine marks the point in

52. Klein, 'Marginalized Victim', pp. 86-87.
53. M. Tsevat, 'Was Samuel a Nazirite?', in M. Fishbane and E. Tov (eds.), *'Sha'arei Talmon': Studies in the Bible, Qumran and the Ancient Near East* (Winona Lake, IN: Eisenbrauns, 1992), pp. 199-204.

the story when she took matters into her own hands and her leadership began to emerge. And she reversed roles with Eli, insofar as he was the one who ought to have reassured her, not the other way around.

Characterization through Speech and Silence
Speech plays a significant part in the Hannah narrative. Hannah spoke first to God, silently but in the public shrine, then to Eli in response to his request that she leave. When Samuel was born she named him with the explanation, 'I have asked him of the Lord' (1 Sam. 1.20). She explained to Elkanah her plans not to go on the annual trip to Shiloh until Samuel was old enough to remain there, she spoke to Eli about her vow and its fulfillment, and she sang her Song. These speeches are remarkable in several ways: she spoke more words than any other barren mother. Her words all concerned her vow and its fulfillment. In fact, grammatically she is the subject of a verb more frequently than she is the object. She uses direct speech in every conversation in ch. 1. In fact, she is the only character to speak in each of these episodes. And she uses poetry to express herself. This distinguishes her within the narrative, as the only other person in 1 Samuel to use poetry is Samuel in 15.22-23.[54]

Equally remarkable are the words Hannah did not speak. She did not respond to Peninnah's taunts, did not answer her husband's four questions (only the last of which gave her an opportunity to reply). She did respond to Eli's request that she leave the shrine, but in so doing she corrected the record about her condition and her business at the shrine. Most remarkable of all is her Song, because of its uniqueness among the barren mother narratives and in fact, among all the biblical narratives involving women.

Another of her verbal actions was to name her son. Hannah was not the only barren mother who named her son. The biblical record indicates that other mothers did, too. 'They named him Esau' (Gen. 25.25 does not specify precisely who named him; one supposes it was his parents. Leah named all her children: Reuben, Simeon, probably Levi, and Judah, Issachar, Zebulun and Dinah as well as Zilpah's sons Gad and Asher. Rachel named her maid Bilhah's sons Dan and Naphthali and her own sons Joseph and Benoni, whose name Jacob changed to Benjamin (29.31–30.24; 35.18). And in Samson's case 'the woman bore

---

54. Meyers, 'Hannah Narrative', p. 122.

a son, and named him Samson' (Judg. 13.24). The naming of a child by the mother does not occur in the Priestly narratives or generational chains. But in the narratives dealing with the premonarchic period of Israel's history, the role of women in naming children is apparently indicative of an authoritative social role, at least within the family, since the child receiving the name comes under the namegiver's influence and control.[55] Maternal naming is found among women in patrilocal societies.[56]

Another point with regard to naming is that Hannah herself is named, and her name appears 14 times in the text. This is significant, considering that women's names comprise only 8 per cent of the names in the Hebrew Bible. The women who are named most frequently are the matriarchs: Sarah's name occurs 55 times; Rebekah's, 30; Rachel's, 46; and Leah's, 34. It is also noteworthy that the matriarchs' importance lies precisely in their maternal function and role. No other women are named with the same frequency as the matriarchs; outside the book of Genesis only Michal (16 times) and Miriam (15 times) are mentioned more often than Hannah. Many other biblical women are mentioned but not named. This is the case with three of the barren mothers: Samson's mother, the Shunammite woman and the woman in Ezra's vision.[57]

The fact that Hannah sang the Song also figures as a unique aspect of the Hannah narrative because Hannah was the only barren mother who made a lengthy speech. And what is more, she did so in a public place. The other women's words were significantly more limited. As I mentioned above several of the women named their sons. And two of the mothers commented on their situations. When Isaac was born Sarah said to Abraham, 'Who would ever have said to Abraham that Sarah would nurse children? Yet I have borne him a son in his old age' (Gen. 21.7). And the woman in Ezra's vision explained, 'After thirty years God heard your handmaid, and looked upon my low estate, and considered my distress, and gave me a son. And I rejoiced greatly over him, I and my husband and all my neighbors; and we gave great glory to the Mighty One' (2 Esd. 9.45). But Hannah sang in praise of God at the Shiloh shrine at pilgrimage time.

55. Meyers, 'Hannah Narrative', p. 121.
56. Jobling, 'What, if Anything', pp. 28-29.
57. Meyers, 'Hannah Narrative', p. 120.

Time and Place

The setting of the story also helps focus on Hannah's uniqueness. Most of the action in the narrative occurs at the Shiloh shrine. And the action in only three and one-half verses (19b-20, 22-23) took place at the family home.

Time was reckoned in the narrative according to the yearly trips to Shiloh, and both second sections mention the זבח (sacrifice) Elkanah offered there. The third section in each part records Hannah's vow and its fulfillment: she offered her first-fruits, just as did Elkanah.

Sight and Insight

Sight and insight play a telling role in the narrative as well. Eli was unable to see that Hannah prayed to the Lord of hosts to look on her misery. So Eli's inability to see was not an obstacle to overcome, but rather a narrative signal that Hannah was following her own rhythms, not those of the people surrounding her. The motif of sight develops further when Hannah informed her husband that she would take her son to the shrine after he was weaned, 'that he may appear in the presence of the Lord, and remain there forever' (1.22).

In his inability to see, Eli functioned in the narrative as a foil, as did Elkanah, for the Lord, who did understand. Likewise, the obnoxious Peninnah was a foil for Hannah, who was dignified and gracious in her action and discourse.[58]

Hannah's Person and Role

The three individuals with whom Hannah interacts throughout the story contribute to marginalizing her emotionally. The three are Peninnah, Elkanah and Eli. Klein analyzes the dynamics of the narrative in terms of R. Girard's notion of mimetic desire. She concludes that Hannah's avoidance of the dynamics of mimetic desire results in her becoming the social ideal. That is, she makes the interaction more socially acceptable, hence becoming the 'social redeemer' to which the title refers. And Hannah's relationship with YHWH sustains her above and beyond the marginalization caused by the three humans. 'Her strength of character renders her the noble core of the narrative: she evolves from Other into paradigm, model of woman, and redeems her family from mimetic desire.'[59]

58. Klein, 'Marginalized Victim', p. 91.
59. Klein, 'Marginalized Victim', p. 92; T. Linafelt, 'Taking Women in

All in all, the narrative portrays Hannah as a bold, determined, dominating woman who wants 'a son *in the service of YHWH*, a son being prepared for a position of leadership in Israel. Perhaps this is an ambitious woman who, having little scope herself, expresses her ambition vicariously through her son'.[60]

Hannah's actions in the narrative affirm her pivotal role in the reform of the priesthood and the transition to the monarchy. After Samuel was weaned she returned with him to the Shiloh shrine, leaving him in Eli's care in fulfillment of her vow. While at the shrine she praised the God who exercises dominion over all.

But her actions and those of others call attention to the struggles inherent in the nascent monarchy. Among these were the need to balance the powers and duties of the king with those of priest and prophet. Eli's lack of hospitality to Hannah on her first visit to the Shiloh shrine, and his lack of understanding of Hannah's purpose and actions at the shrine, create tension regarding the office and role of the priesthood. The narrative develops the tension further in its description of the corruption of Eli's sons (2.12-17) and of Samuel's increasing favor in the divine eyes (v. 26). Samuel anointed Saul and David in a priestly ritual (10.1; 16.13). And throughout the reigns of the two kings the struggles over who would perform priestly duties illustrate the kingdom's efforts to balance the powers of priest and king (1 Sam. 3.8-14; 2 Sam. 6.12-13).

Samuel's own resistance to the people's initial request for a king, and his opposition to the divine decision to replace Saul as king, serve to define the prophetic role in the monarchy. As intermediary between the people and God, Samuel voiced requests and positions with which he personally disagreed, and carried out divine directions that he found disagreeable. These events illustrate the struggle to balance powers within the nascent monarchy, and the divine dominion that prevailed.

At the end of the Samuel corpus, David's Song of Thanks (2 Sam. 22) acknowledges that the divine king was Israel's ultimate leader, and his final testament (23.1-7) offers the reflections of a God-fearing and righteous king whose personal life and political dynasty were guided by

Samuel: Readers/Responses/Responsibility', in D.N. Fewell (ed.), *Reading Between Texts: Intertextuality and the Hebrew Bible* (Literary Currents in Biblical Interpretation; Louisville: Westminster/John Knox Press, 1992), pp. 99-113 (107-108).

60. Jobling, 'Hannah's Desire', p. 132.

the divine Spirit.[61] These words of Hannah at the beginning, and of David at the end, envelop the Samuel corpus and the early monarchy within the programmatic theme of divine dominion over the people, through the specific instrumentality of the kings anointed by Hannah's son.

This discussion of the biblical story and its narrative and historical contexts offers a backdrop against which to examine the three later works, which I will take up in the following three chapters.

---

61. W. Harrelson, 'Creative Spirit in the Old Testament: A Study of the Last Words of David (2 Sam. 23.1-7)', in D. Durkin, OSB (ed.), *Sin, Salvation, and the Spirit* (Collegeville, MN: Liturgical Press, 1979), pp. 127-33 (131).

Chapter 3

PSEUDO-PHILO'S STORY OF HANNAH IN *BIBLICAL ANTIQUITIES*

Biblical Antiquities (Bib. Ant.) is a rewritten Bible, a work that expands the biblical narrative by adding various details such as oral legends, lessons important to the community, or items to catch the reader's attention. Rewritten Bibles are thought to have been used in synagogues for teaching purposes. *Biblical Antiquities* recounts the biblical narrative from the time of Adam to the death of Saul. Its expansions of the Hannah narrative and Song are the focus of this chapter. Other examples of expansion include *Antiquities of the Jews (Ant.)* of Josephus and the book of *Jubilees*. And *Targum of the Prophets*, which I will discuss in the following chapter, enlarges the Song into a prediction of divine guidance throughout Israel's early military history.

The Text, its Date and Provenance

Little is known with certainty about the language and date of composition of the work and its place of origin. But logical deductions have been made based on the text.

Textual Issues

Although no extant copies of *Biblical Antiquities* are known in Hebrew, that was probably the language of composition. Various Semitisms in the Latin text, errors in translation and independence from the Greek Hebrew Bible support that hypothesis. The work is not likely to have been composed in Aramaic, primarily because several translation errors can be explained from Hebrew vocabulary but not from Aramaic. The extant Latin versions are the earliest known today, and are most likely translations from Greek, into which the original Hebrew was translated. The biblical quotations in the Latin versions follow the Vulgate in some instances and the Septuagint in others.[1]

---

1.   D.J. Harrington in D.J. Harrington, C. Perrot and P.-M. Bogaert, *Pseudo-Philon: Les Antiquités bibliques*, II (Paris: Cerf, 1976), pp. 75-77; C. Perrot in

Date and Provenance

Opinion is divided as to whether *Biblical Antiquities* was composed before or after 70 CE. Those who favor the earlier date point to the book's rewritten Bible genre, which fell into disuse after 70 CE; and the references to sacrifice, for example, Abraham's words to Isaac, 'Behold now, my son, I am offering you as a holocaust and am delivering you into the hands that gave you to me' (32.3); and references to the Temple, for instance, 'Now at the new altar that was in Gilgal Joshua had decreed even unto this day what holocausts would be offered every year by the sons of Israel' (22.8). These references suggest to advocates of the pre-70 date that the Temple was still standing at the time of composition. But others note the book's literary parallels to *2 Baruch* and *4 Ezra*, in spite of their different theological concerns. They use this information to support the later date of composition. In either case, the work must have been composed no later than around 100 CE because the biblical text on which the author relied was, according to F.M. Cross's categories, Palestinian rather than Babylonian or Egyptian. Palestinian texts were probably suppressed around 100 CE. And it was probably composed no earlier than around 135 BCE if the reference to Getal, king of the sons of Ammon, in 39.8 refers to Zenon, ruler of Philadelphia (Ammon).[2]

Several factors point to Palestine as the book's most likely place of composition. For example, it was originally composed in Hebrew, it depends on the Palestinian biblical text, and it expresses concern for Temple-related issues. The anonymous author is known as *Pseudo-Philo*, but the work differs from that of Philo in several ways. Its use of the Bible differs from Philo's, and it contradicts Philo's work in several instances. In addition, Philo does not seem to have known the Hebrew language well enough to compose in Hebrew.[3]

The community within which *Biblical Antiquities* was composed seems, from the perspective of the book, to have been a group of

C. Perrot, and P.-M. Bogaert, with the collaboration of D.J. Harrington, *Pseudo-Philon: Les Antiquités bibliques*, I (Paris: Cerf, 1976), pp. 15-57.

2. P.-M. Bogaert in Harrington, *Pseudo-Philon*, pp. 66-74. D.J. Harrington discusses this question further in 'Pseudo-Philo', in *OTP*, II, pp. 297-377 (299); see also F.M. Cross, Jr. 'The History of the Biblical Text in the Light of the Discoveries in the Judaean Desert', *HTR* 57 (1964), pp. 281-99.

3. See Harrington, 'Pseudo-Philo', pp. 299-300.

Pharisaic Jews in Palestine.[4] The political setting seems to be the period shortly before the Roman destruction of the Temple in 70 CE, leading me to support the earlier pre-70 date of composition.

Women in Biblical Antiquities

One of the remarkable features of the work is its interpretations of biblical women. It adds much genealogical information about women in the primeval history and the account of the judges, but almost none in the ancestral history. It also adds predictions by or about women. Several of these give information that would already have been available to *Pseudo-Philo*'s readers. And two predictions were made by mothers at significant moments in their sons' lives. These predictions offer information about the leaders of the people. Finally, *Biblical Antiquities* adds instructions, often about wisdom topics, given by women. But while the women speak more than in the biblical stories, for the most part they acknowledge a source other than themselves for their authority and their words. It is unclear if that strengthens their status within the community by connecting them with the sources of authority or if it weakens their position. But on the other hand, *Biblical Antiquities* omits or diminishes certain women. For example, Rebekah is not named in *Biblical Antiquities*, and in fact receives only passing mention in 8.4.[5]

These changes from the biblical version have led to speculation about the role of women in *Pseudo-Philo*'s community, including the possibility of female authorship of the book. The question is a complex one, and several approaches have been taken in an effort to answer it. For example, Pieter van der Horst concludes from his study of the women in the *Testament of Job* that the final seven chapters of the work must have been composed by a woman because the masculine and feminine roles are completely reversed in that section of the work. He observes, 'Women are the leaders, the persons with insight and spiritual gifts, while the men, on the contrary, are just the reverse.'[6] But his brief

4.   F.J. Murphy: *Pseudo-Philo: Rewriting the Bible* (New York: Oxford University Press, 1993), p. 7.

5.   For a catalogue of the changes regarding women in the text, see J.E. Cook, 'Females and the Feminine in Pseudo-Philo', in *Proceedings: Eastern Great Lakes and Midwest Biblical Societies* 13 (1993), pp. 151-59.

6.   P.W. van der Horst, 'Portraits of Women in Pseudo-Philo', *JSP* 5 (1989),

analysis of the women in *Pseudo-Philo* leads him to observe frequent expansions of women without a corresponding lessening of the importance or quality of men. He concludes that it is not possible to assert that the author was a woman, but:

> we surely have to establish that the portraits of a number of biblical women in *Biblical Antiquities* are of such a nature as to point in the direction of an author who was concerned, among other things, to ascribe to women a greater and much more important role in Israel's history than they were accorded in the Bible... That he–she did this with an eye on his–her actual situation can hardly be doubted, and this is a point where further research is to be done.[7]

The question cannot be answered with certainty at this time, but it invites speculation about the community in which *Biblical Antiquities* was written. Perhaps the synagogal congregation for whom the book was composed expected to hear eschatological instruction from the mouths of women, the givers and enlighteners of life. Or perhaps women hoped for opportunities to offer such teaching. Either possibility might imply that the listening congregation acknowledged and respected women as wise teachers of the community, or that such was the hope of the women in the congregation.

Theological Themes in the Work

The entire work highlights divine guidance of the Israelite people, particularly their leaders, throughout their early history. Divine protection during the period of the judges receives special attention in the work, perhaps in reflection of the people's subjection to Rome at the time when *Biblical Antiquities* was written.[8] In fact, the Hannah narrative is introduced with the people's request for a judge who would rule in the spirit of Kenaz, the first and ideal judge. When God promised a son to be born of Elkanah's sterile wife who would rule over the people, they

p. 29-46 (45). See also K.L. King, 'Sophia and Christ in the *Apocryphon of John*', in *idem* (ed.), *Images of the Feminine in Gnosticism* (Philadelphia: Fortress Press, 1988), pp. 158-76 (158-59); R.S. Kraemer, 'Women's Authorship of Jewish and Christian Literature in the Greco-Roman Period', in A.J. Levine (ed.), *'Women Like This': New Perspectives on Jewish Women in the Greco–Roman World* (Atlanta: Scholars Press, 1991), pp. 221-42.

7.   Van der Horst, 'Portraits', pp. 45-46.

8.   Murphy, *Rewriting*, p. 264.

responded, 'Behold perhaps now God has remembered us so as to free us from the hand of those who hate us' (49.8).

Divine guidance extends in a particular way to the religious leaders. For example, *Biblical Antiquities* omits the power struggle between Moses and Korah (Num. 16.15-19), focusing instead on divine initiative. God predicts about Korah and his followers, 'Hell will no longer spit them back, and their destruction will not be remembered' (*Bib. Ant.* 16.3). In another example the narrative enhances the role of Eli the priest in chs. 49–54. This focus on divine protection is easily understood in the context of the Roman occupation and control of civil life in the Second Temple period.[9]

The covenant figures prominently in *Biblical Antiquities*, as does the reward-retribution cycle. It is extended to include judgment at death as well as an afterlife. These eschatological themes are particularly prominent in the Song of Hannah in 51.3-6, Deborah's hymn in 32.3, and Jonathan's words to David in 62.9. The words reflect the community's questions about the nature of life after death such as whether all or only some people are evil, whether all people will die or only the evil ones, and whether the good will actually be raised from the dead or will be transformed from earthly existence into another mode of life.[10] Each of these themes appears in the Hannah narrative, and will be discussed in greater detail below in the analysis of the text.

The Hannah Story in Biblical Antiquities

The narrative is found in chs. 49–51 and can be divided into four episodes. These include: first, Elkanah's selection as judge and his refusal to accept the appointment (ch. 49); second, Hannah's request for a son, and the birth and dedication of Samuel by Hannah (50.1–51.3a); third, the Song of Hannah (51.3b-6); and fourth, Samuel's anointing by the people (51.7).

The first part of the narrative emphasizes Samuel's bridge position between the judges and the kings. *Biblical Antiquities* expands the

---

9. G.W.E. Nickelsburg, 'Good and Bad Leaders in Pseudo-Philo's *Liber Antiquitatum Biblicarum*', in G.W.E. Nickelsburg and J.J. Collins (eds.), *Ideal Figures in Ancient Judaism: Profiles and Paradigms* (Chico, CA: Scholars Press, 1980), pp. 49-65.

10. See C. Perrot's comprehensive treatment of the book's theological themes in Harrington, *Pseudo-Philon*, II, pp. 39-65.

beginning of the biblical narrative to include casting lots for a new judge. The people cast lots four times until finally Elkanah is designated. The procedure links Elkanah with the first judge, Kenaz, whom the people chose by lot after Joshua's death, as directed by the angel of the Lord (25.2). Josephus (*Ant.* 5.3.3. §182) also identifies him as Israel's first judge. But Judg. 3.9 identifies Othniel, son of Kenaz, as the first judge. From then on the people respect Kenaz as the model judge.[11]

Elkanah, however, declines the appointment rather than take on himself the sins of the people (49.5).[12] Consequently God promises that Elkanah's son will rule and prophesy (49.7).

When the people ask which of Peninnah's ten sons will be chosen, God responds that none of her sons can rule; the son will be born from his sterile wife. The divine promise 'I will love him as I have loved Isaac' (49.8) also introduces the motifs of love and remembrance that figure prominently throughout this narrative segment.

The casting of lots serves as a connector on several levels in the story. It links the final judge, Samuel, with the first, Kenaz, and introduces the announcement of the next ruler, who serves by divine appointment as both ruler and prophet. And it foreshadows Hannah's and Samuel's entrance into the story.

The second episode relates directly to the biblical account of Hannah while expanding on Peninnah's taunts, Elkanah's efforts to reassure Hannah, Hannah's prayer for a son, Eli's priestly reassurance, and the birth and dedication of Samuel.

In the biblical account Peninnah remains silent, except that the narrator repeats that she provoked her rival wife, to irritate her on account of her sterility. *Biblical Antiquities* expands on Peninnah's taunts, putting into her mouth words that underscore her rivalry with Hannah. Peninnah's words play on the love motif introduced above, 'I know that my husband will love me, because he delights in the sight of my sons standing around him...' and 'When among women the fruit of her womb is not so, love would have been in vain' (50.1-2).

Elkanah reassures Hannah with questions similar to those in the biblical account, but his fourth question substitutes 'Are not your ways of

11. Harrington offers a detailed discussion of the relation of *Biblical Antiquities* to canonical and apocryphal works in 'Pseudo-Philo', pp. 301-302.

12. Harrington, *Pseudo-Philon*, II, p. 212.

behaving better than the ten sons of Peninnah?' (50.3) for the biblical query about Hannah's love for him, a curious substitution in light of Peninnah's taunts.[13]

Hannah's prayer for a son differs sharply from her biblical vow to return the desired son to the Lord. *Pseudo-Philo* recounts that Hannah requests a son as a reward for her righteousness, and that she prays silently in her perceived unworthiness to be heard and to avoid further tormenting from Peninnah. In her request she refers not to the love motif but to the notion of wealth in her plea, 'Perhaps I am not worthy to be heard, and Peninnah will then be even more eager to taunt me as she does daily when she says, "where is your God in whom you trust?" I know that neither she who has many sons is rich nor she who has few is poor' (50.5). There is no vow or foreshadowing of the evil behavior of Eli's sons in *Biblical Antiquities*

Eli the priest reassures Hannah in a significantly expanded form in *Biblical Antiquities*, from the biblical uncomprehending generic blessing to the invitation 'Tell me why you are being taunted'. Hannah responds by telling Eli of her desire for a son to which he replies, 'Go, because I know for what you have prayed; your prayer has been heard' (50.7). *Pseudo-Philo* goes on to report, 'But Eli the priest did not want to tell her that a prophet had been foreordained to be born from her. For he had heard that when the Lord spoke concerning him' (50.8). *Pseudo-Philo* explicitly links Eli with the priestly line when he identifies him as the son of Phinehas, son of Eleazar. He is thus Aaron's great-grandson (see Exod. 6.25).

The actual narration of Samuel's birth eliminates Elkanah altogether. It interprets Samuel's name differently from the biblical account: instead of 'I have asked him of the Lord', *Pseudo-Philo* offers 'Mighty One', and credits God, rather than Hannah with naming the child in another departure from the biblical account.

Next, the dedication of Samuel takes on a different tone in *Pseudo-Philo*'s account. Since Hannah had made no vow to return him to the Lord, there is no question here of fulfilling a promise. And since Elkanah is absent from the account, there is no discussion about waiting until Samuel is weaned, before taking him to Shiloh. *Biblical Antiquities* merely states that she nursed him for two years, then weaned him,

---

13. Harrington suggests emending the Latin *mores* to *amores* in *Pseudo-Philon*, II, p. 214.

took him to Shiloh, and placed him before Eli. When she identifies her child to him as the one she had requested, she learns from Eli that Samuel's birth had been promised earlier to the people (51.2). Then Eli explains that the boy's birth served the additional function of legitimating Hannah as a teacher of wisdom, after which the narrative relates, 'On hearing this Hannah prayed and said' (51.3).

The third episode is the Song of Hannah, which differs significantly in form and content from the biblical version. I will consider the Song in detail following this general discussion of the four episodes.

Episode four takes place after the Song, expanding and modifying the biblical version. The text states that after 'they' (the antecedent is ambiguous) leave Shiloh, 'the people' bring Samuel to Eli at Shiloh, anoint the boy and express the hope, 'Let the prophet live among the people, and may he be a light to this nation for a long time!' (*Bib. Ant.* 51.7). The text has a celebratory tone, describing their leave-taking 'with gladness, rejoicing and exulting in heart' and the people's arrival at Shiloh 'with timbrels and dances, lutes and harps'. The cause of their joy was 'the glory God had worked with them'. (It is unclear whether 'their' refers to Hannah and Elkanah, as we would expect, but Elkanah is not mentioned as making this trip; or to Hannah and Samuel, which would follow from 51.1 and from the narrator's comment that the people brought Samuel to Eli; or to the people in general, who had anticipated Samuel's birth from the time of the divine promise in 49.8.)

The people's elation results from the divine gift of a prophet to them. They anoint him in the presence of Eli and the Lord. They then express their hope for him and for themselves in the words of blessing, 'Let the prophet live among the people, and may he be a light to this nation for a long time!' (51.7).

These expansions cast Samuel as a public figure from the time his mother takes him to Shiloh. Eli identifies him as the one promised to the tribes, and identifies Hannah as their source of wisdom. Then Eli witnesses Samuel's anointing by the people.

Now I will return to a discussion of the Song.

Pseudo-Philo's *Song of Hannah*

The Song of Hannah appears in the same context as the biblical version, in the account of Hannah's dedication of Samuel at the Shiloh shrine after she weaned him. My translation follows.[14]

51.3   And Hannah prayed,[15] 'Come to my voice, all nations, and listen to my speech, all kingdoms, because my mouth has been opened to speak,[16] and my lips have been commanded to sing a hymn to the Lord. Drip, my breasts, and proclaim your testimony, because you have been commanded to give milk. For the one who is filled with your milk[17] will be established, and the people will be illuminated by his words, and to the nations he will show the ordinances,[18] and his horn will be exalted[19] very high.

4   Therefore I will speak my words openly, because from me will come forth the ordering[20] of the Lord, and all people will learn the truth.[21] Do not hasten to say great things or to let lofty words come forth from your mouth,[22] but take delight in glorifying [God]. For when the light from which wisdom is born comes forth, not those who possess many things will be called wealthy, nor will those who have borne in abundance be called mothers. For the barren one who has given birth has been filled, but the one with many children has been emptied.[23]

5   For the Lord puts to death in judgment and brings to life in mercy.[24] For the evil ones live in this world, and he gives life to the just when he wills. For he confines the evil ones in darkness, and preserves his light for the just. And when the evil ones die they will

---

14. The following translation is my own, and also appears in J.E. Cook, 'The Song of Hannah in Pseudo-Philo's *Biblical Antiquities*', in M. Kiley (ed.), *Prayer from Alexander to Constantine: A Critical Anthology* (New York: Routledge, 1997), pp. 73-78 (76).

15. These words occur verbatim in 1 Sam. 2.1.

16. The Latin reads, *ut loquar*, 'that I may speak'.

17. The Latin reads, *qui lactatur de vobis*, 'who is given milk by you'.

18. The Latin word *terminos* can be traced back to the Hebrew חוקים, 'limits, boundaries, laws, statutes'. It occurs in *Biblical Antiquities* both here and in 15.6. See Harrington, 'Pseudo-Philo', p. 323 n. 15d. The word 'ordinances' highlights the relationship between that word and 'ordering' in the following verse. (See n. 20 below.)

19. These words are similar to 1 Sam. 2.10.

20. The Latin reads *constitutio*. (See n. 18 above).

21. These words allude to Isa. 51.4.

22. These words are similar to 1 Sam. 2.3.

23. These words are similar to 1 Sam. 2.5. See also Harrington's note that the Latin depends on the Hebrew שבעה of 1 Sam. 2.5, which alludes to the number 'seven' in 'Pseudo-Philo', p. 365.

24. These words are an expansion of 1 Sam. 2.6.

perish, but when the just go to sleep they will be set free.[25] In this way every judgment will remain until the one who upholds it is revealed.

6   Speak, speak, Hannah, and do not be silent; sing a hymn, daughter of Batuel, about the marvelous things that God has performed with you. Who is Hannah that a prophet is born of her?[26] Or who is the daughter of Batuel that she should give birth to the light of the people?[27] And you, Elkanah, get up and gird your loins;[28] sing a hymn about the signs of the Lord, for Asaph prophesied in the wilderness concerning your son, saying, "Moses and Aaron are among his priests and Samuel is among them".[29] See, the word has been fulfilled according to the prophecy.[30] And these things will endure until the horn is given to his anointed one, and [until] power is present at the throne of his king.[31] So let my son stay here and serve[32] until he is made a light for this nation.'

Hannah begins by inviting all nations and kingdoms to pay attention to the hymn she has been commanded to sing. She then metaphorically invites her breasts to testify, calling them to 'drip' and 'tell'. The two verbs highlight the strong connection between her motherhood and her role as teacher, highlighting the author's understanding that when Hannah's womb was opened, this made her eligible to open her mouth in teaching.

Hannah then speaks, first as the mother of the Giver of Light and Law (51.3-5), then as the mother of Prophet and Priest (v. 6). These two points of view divide Hannah's speech into two parts.

In the first part, the opening words recall the biblical Moses' farewell in Deuteronomy 32. Moses called on heaven and earth to listen to his words that fell like rain. Here Hannah calls on all people to hear the words she speaks in nourishment, like her milk that fed her son Samuel.

---

25. The contrast between the just and the wicked is similar to the opposition between the faithful and the wicked in 1 Sam. 2.9.

26. Literally, 'that a prophet is from her', followed by 'that she gave birth'. This translation respects the parallel meaning, and might also reconcile the similarities in the Greek ἐγενήθη (was) and ἐγεννήθη (was born). See Harrington's note in 'Pseudo-Philo', p. 366 n. 511.

27. These words recall Isa. 51.4.

28. These words are similar to Jer. 1.17 and Job 38.3.

29. These words are similar to Ps. 99.6.

30. Literally, 'the prophecy agrees'.

31. These words are similar to 1 Sam. 2.10.

32. These words are similar to 1 Sam. 2.11.

The words flash back, not only to the biblical Moses, but also to *Pseudo-Philo*'s interpretation of him. *Biblical Antiquities* places Samuel among the leaders whom Moses predicted the people would request after his death, 'But then you and your sons and all your generations will rise up after you and lament the day of my death and say in their heart, "Who will give us another shepherd like Moses or such a judge for the sons of Israel to pray always for our sins and to be heard for our iniquities?"' (*Bib. Ant.* 19.3). The flashback highlights Hannah's role as well: she, like Moses, is impelled to speak to all and to praise the Lord. Her conviction and her new role as mother prompts her to command the attention, not only of her family and friends, but of all nations and kingdoms when she introduces herself as mother of the Giver of Light and Law.

Hannah's message flows not only in words but also in the maternal mode of milk, to nourish with wisdom her son the Giver of Light and Law. She asserts, 'For the one who is filled with your milk will be established, and the people will be illuminated by his words, and to the nations he will show the ordinances' (51.3), thus linking light and law.

Hannah then elaborates on the second of her son's two roles, stating, 'From me will come forth the ordering of the Lord' (51.4). With these words she strengthens the allusion to Moses the Lawgiver, relates her son Samuel to him, and further develops the image by referring to her son as the personification of the Law.[33] In keeping with Samuel's predicted role as the 'light from which wisdom is born' (51.4) he will usher in an age of reversals that Hannah describes in language reminiscent of the biblical Hannah (see 1 Sam. 2.4-9). Wealth and motherhood will take on different meanings, and death will assume new significance, bringing reward or punishment for the way people live. Here Hannah expands the motif of light to include the notion of reward for the just. She contrasts light with darkness to illustrate the consequences of one's life: 'For he confines the evil ones in darkness, and preserves his light for the just (*Bib. Ant.* 51.5). Thus Light and Law take on greater proportions than they previously enjoyed: they offer guidance throughout life, and form the basis of judgment at the time of death. Hannah's words highlight Samuel's pivotal role in ushering in

33. Hebrew תורה, Greek νόμος, Vulgate *constitutio* (M. Philonenko, 'Une Paraphrase du cantique d'Anne', *RHPR* 42 [1962], pp. 157-68 [165]). French *dessein* (Harrington, *Pseudo-Philon*, II, p. 218).

this new dispensation, as well as her own significant position as his mother.

In the second part of the speech Hannah calls on herself as her father Batuel's daughter to speak and sing about the divine miracles on her behalf. The thematic transition from emphasis on her role as Mother of the Giver of Light and Law to Mother of the Priest and Prophet recalls Isa. 51.4: 'for a law will go forth from me, and my justice for a light to the peoples'. Hannah then calls upon her husband to join her in praise because his son's priesthood was prophesied in the wilderness by Elkanah's ancestor Asaph.[34] Samuel's importance will endure until he anoints David king, then he will become the king's servant. Hannah concludes her words with the specific request to leave her son in Eli's care to prepare for his God-given mission.

Form of the Song
The expanded Song is prose rather than poetry, and its genre corresponds more closely to a testament than to a hymn or song of thanks.[35]

Charlesworth's definition of the testamentary genre acknowledges its diversity of content and focuses on the life setting of the testament. The speaker assembles relatives and friends around his deathbed and utters farewell words. These may include exhortations to avoid particular temptations, instructions for righteous living, blessings, curses and predictions for the future.[36] The form appears frequently in intertestamental literature, where we find testaments pronounced by Adam, Abraham, Isaac and Jacob, Jacob's 12 sons, Moses, Solomon and Job. I use the term 'testament' in this broad sense, taking into consideration the life setting Charlesworth describes.

Pseudo-Philo shifts the setting of the testament from the ancestral deathbed to the shrine at Shiloh, when Hannah presents her son Samuel to Eli. This adaptation situates Hannah within the tradition of Israel's leaders while describing a transition to a new type of leadership.

Themes of the Song
In keeping with the Song's testamentary genre, it contains several

34. C. Perrot, *Pseudo-Philon*, I, p. 220.
35. See Cook, 'Text and Contexts', pp. 87-101, for a discussion of the biblical Song's genre.
36. Harrington, 'Pseudo-Philo', p. 773; J.E. Cook, 'Pseudo-Philo's Song of Hannah: Testament of a Mother in Israel', *JSP* 9 (1991), pp. 103-114 (104-106).

teachings that show the concerns of the first-century writer. Among these the most prominent is eschatology; the others, divine guidance of the people, particularly their leaders, and covenant flow from it.

Hannah's teaching on eschatology figures prominently in the first part of the Song, in connection with her comments as Mother of the Giver of Light and Law. Her words broaden the significance of death into a bridge between past and future. It is the moment that defines one's life, when the Lord judges the wicked, condemning them to darkness and death; but shows mercy to the just, rewarding them with light and life. In eschatological terms darkness represents imprisonment while light is freedom. And this theme highlights the importance of faithfulness to the covenant, not only for this life but also for the next. But at the same time it makes clear that all have access to knowledge about how to live justly.

Several subtleties relate this text to other works of the time, and illustrate the common struggle to come to terms with the meaning of death. One of these is the actual event itself: *Pseudo-Philo* implies that only the wicked actually die. He states that the Lord kills the wicked, and that 'when the evil ones die, then they will perish, but when the just go to sleep they will be set free'. *Pseudo-Philo* also suggests two times of judgment, the first at the individual's death, which will remain until the one who upholds it will be revealed'. The exact time of this second moment of judgment remains imprecise (see 2 Thess. 2.6-12). The geographical locations of punishment and reward are not specified, except that punishment will be in darkness while reward will be in the light. In eschatological terms darkness represents imprisonment while light is freedom.

Judgment is related to mercy, broadening the meaning of these contrasting motifs beyond wisdom and the lack of it, to include reward and punishment after death: 'For he confines the evil ones in darkness, and preserves his light for the just' (*Bib. Ant.* 51.5). Then Hannah specifies the eschatological meaning of darkness and light: darkness equals imprisonment while light is freedom.

Hannah nuances her teaching of two steps in the judgment process, the unpredictable time of divine mercy, and the qualitative difference in the fate of the wicked and the just: the wicked one's death is definitive while the just one's sleep results in freedom.

Hannah's teaching builds on the theme of covenant by highlighting the importance of just actions. But it also makes clear that knowledge of what is right is available to everyone, underscoring the theme of divine guidance of all the people. She refers specifically to divine actions on her own behalf: 'Sing a hymn, daughter of Batuel, about the marvelous things that God has performed with you' (51.6). She follows those words with particular reference to the miracle of Samuel, 'Who is Hannah that a prophet is born of her?' in answer to her petition, 'because God has shut up my womb, I have prayed before him that I do not go forth from this world without fruit and that I do not die without having my own image' (50.7). In fact she had already been chosen to be the mother of the prophet who would lead the people, as God explains earlier, 'None of the sons of Peninnah can rule the people, but the one who is born from the sterile woman whom I have given to [Elkanah] as a wife will be a prophet before me' (49.8).

But divine guidance extends to all people and events, as she makes clear in her assertion, 'The Lord puts to death in judgment and brings to life in mercy' (51.5). One of the ways God takes care of everyone is by offering special guidance to the leaders ('For the one who is filled with your milk will be established, and the people will be illuminated by his words,' 51.3).

After this detailed look at Hannah's words at the shrine, we return to the entire story. I will discuss it first in relation to the barren mother type, then in terms of its two simultaneous plots, public and private. Finally I will discuss the characterization in the story and its effect on the overall themes of *Pseudo-Philo*'s Hannah story.

The Barren Mother Type in Biblical Antiquities

If we consider the plot according to the variations on the type of the barren mother, we can identify several significant features. Like the biblical account, it fits the competition model, but intensifies it by adding descriptive details. For instance, instead of merely reporting that Peninnah taunted Hannah, *Biblical Antiquities* quotes her on two occasions. She teases, 'What does it profit you that Elkanah your husband loves you, for you are a dry tree? And I know that my husband will love me, because he delights in the sight of my sons standing around him like a plantation of olive trees' (50.1). Then she says, 'A wife is not really loved even if her husband loves her or her beauty. Let Hannah not boast in her appearance; but she who boasts, let her boast when she sees her offspring before her. And when among women the fruit of her womb is not so, love will be in vain. For what did it profit Rachel that Jacob loved her? And unless the fruit of her womb had been given to him, his love would have been in vain' (50.2). The narrative indicates that Peninnah issued these taunts daily, as opposed to the biblical yearly slurs. Elkanah refers explicitly to the competition in his embellished question, 'Are not your ways of behaving better than the ten sons of Peninnah?' (50.3). And when Hannah prays for a son, she, too, refers to the competition, 'Perhaps I am not worthy to be heard, and Peninnah will then be even more eager to taunt me as she does daily...' (50.5). But like the biblical account, *Biblical Antiquities* does not engage Hannah directly in competition with Peninnah.

Eli at first accuses her of drunkenness, as in the biblical account. But *Biblical Antiquities* revises the scene in the Shiloh shrine, having Hannah explain to Eli the reason for her sadness. Eli sends her on her way with assurances that her prayer has been heard. But reversing the biblical version, Eli and not Hannah knows the nature of the promise. And he withholds from her the information that a son has already been promised to her. (In *Biblical Antiquities* Hannah seems to be the only person in the narrative who does not know that a son has been promised to her.) *Pseudo-Philo* does not report births of any other children to Hannah, in contrast to the biblical account.

In terms of the promise model, *Biblical Antiquities* contrasts with the biblical account, in which the childless Hannah goes to Shiloh and promises that if God grants her a child, she will return the child to God. But *Biblical Antiquities*'s version remains more faithful to the promise model than does the biblical account, in which Hannah alone makes the promise to God. In all the other biblical promise narratives, the promise is made by the Deity or a divine messenger. In *Biblical Antiquities* the Lord promises all the people that Elkanah's son will rule over them. The people initially question the divine promise, not doubting the promise itself but rather clarifying which of Peninnah's sons the Lord intends as their leader (49.8). God clarifies the promise with the announcement that none of Peninnah's ten sons can rule. Rather, a son will be given to Elkanah's other wife, who is sterile (49.8). God tells the people, 'None of the sons of Peninnah can rule the people, but the one who is born from the sterile woman whom I have given to him as a wife will be a prophet before me' (49.8). The narrative later implies that Hannah is unaware of the divine promise; she learns of it only after Samuel's birth (51.2).

Then, as in the biblical narrative, doubt is expressed by Eli in thinking that Hannah is drunk. But he does not doubt the promise itself. He does, however, vary the confirmation element by not referring to the divine promise, telling Hannah only that her prayer has been heard (50.7). *Pseudo-Philo* records that Hannah named her child Samuel, as God had said, even though Hannah was unaware of the promise. *Biblical Antiquities* interprets the name, 'mighty one' (51.1).

Biblical Antiquities includes the request model as well, but in a more complex way than the biblical narrative. Two requests are made, one by all the people who ask for a leader (49.6), and the other by Hannah whose prayer to God implies rather than states a request for a son (50.4-5). The divine response to all the people comes directly in an explicit promise that Hannah will bear the child who will serve (49.8). But the response to Hannah comes only in Eli's assurance that her prayer has been heard (50.7).

The Story's Two Plots

Each of the barren mother models highlights a puzzling feature of *Pseudo-Philo*'s version, the fact the Hannah was the only one who was unaware of the divine promise that she would bear a son to rule the people. That aspect of the plot actually creates two plots in *Biblical Antiquities*, public and private.[37] In the public plot all the people asked for a leader, received the divine promise that Elkanah's 'other wife' the 'sterile woman' (49.8) would bear a son to rule, and finally anointed Samuel at Shiloh. In the private plot, Hannah asked God for a child to vindicate her righteousness, told Eli of her desire to have a child in her image, bore the child and gave him the name chosen by God, eventually took the child to Eli, and then learned from him what everyone else already knew, that Samuel had been promised to the people. She learned further that Samuel's birth made her the mother, not merely of a son, but of all Israel. Eli's announcement commissioned her to praise God in words that explicitly praised God for making her the mother of the people. Her hymn brought together the public and private plots, interweaving them into a single story and highlighting the public plot.

37. Jobling sees public and private plots in the biblical version in 'Hannah's Desire', pp. 131-42 (136).

Unique Features of the Narrative

Pseudo-Philo's reworking of the story results in several features that distinguish the narrative from the biblical account. These include the two simultaneous plots, particularities of characterization, the 'love' motif and the eventual merging of the two plots. I will discuss each of these in turn.

Characterization in the Story

The two simultaneous plots with their greater and lesser importance are supported by the characterization in the narrative. Hannah is initially portrayed as God-fearing from her youth, but her prayer for a child lacks the personal authority of the biblical Hannah's vow. It reveals only her desperation, fueled by Peninnah's taunts, at being childless. And without Hannah's knowledge, Samuel was already promised to the people; hence Hannah's request is really superfluous. The fact that the reader, narrator and other characters in the narrative already anticipate Samuel's birth while Peninnah taunts Hannah about her childlessness and Hannah begs for a son to take away her disgrace detracts further from her personal authority. After Samuel's birth Hannah assumes a position of greater authority in the community than did the biblical Hannah, by reason of her explicit maternal nurturing of all Israel. But again this results directly from Eli's words rather than from Hannah's own sense of herself. Finally, episode four of the narrative highlights yet again Hannah's diminished personal authority by reporting that the people bring Samuel to Eli at Shiloh, anoint him and bless him as a prophet and light to the nation. Hannah's role in making Samuel a leader is completely eliminated by *Pseudo-Philo*.

Hannah is intimidated by Peninnah's taunts in *Biblical Antiquities* She prays silently for a child because, as she says, 'Perhaps I am not worthy to be heard, and Peninnah will then be even more eager to taunt me as she does daily' (50.5).

And Hannah appears more deferential to Eli in *Biblical Antiquities* While in the biblical narrative she does not tell him of her request for a son, in *Biblical Antiquities* she accepts his invitation to tell him why she is being taunted. (*Biblical Antiquities* does not specify how Eli knows of that difficulty. It apparently bases Eli's insight on Hannah's words in the biblical version.)

Peninnah is more defined as an abrasive rival in *Biblical Antiquities* than in the biblical account, because *Pseudo-Philo* records her taunts as direct speech. And *Pseudo-Philo* suggests that Peninnah's taunts affect Hannah more than does the biblical account. For example, 'And so it was when she was taunting her daily, and Hannah was saddened very much' (50.2). These details highlight the tension between the two women, and depict Hannah as a more realistic character. These details might well have been added to catch the attention of *Pseudo-Philo's* synagogue audience, in preparation for the teaching that would follow in the Song.

Eli is more knowledgeable in *Biblical Antiquities* than in the Bible. His biblical lack of sight and insight is downplayed. While he mistakes Hannah's disturbance for a sign of drunkenness, he knows something about her that she herself does not know. And he withholds it from her, in spite of the fact that the information that she will bear a son would gives her the very reassurance that she seeks. Later in *Biblical Antiquities*, Eli takes a stronger stand in reprimanding his sons for their abuse of the priesthood than in the biblical account (52.2-3; cf. 1 Sam. 2.23-25). *Biblical Antiquities* does not repeat the biblical note that Eli's eyesight was failing (1 Sam. 3.2) or that he waits by the side of the road, waiting to hear news of the battle because he is blind (1 Sam. 4.14-15).

But when Hannah brings the two-year-old Samuel to Eli, he finally gives her the information of which she alone is unaware: he tells her that the child is not simply an answer to her request, but on a larger scale he has already been promised to the people. He then legitimates her as nurturer of all Israel, after which Hannah prays her Song. Eli's knowledge in contrast to Hannah's ignorance, and Eli's eventual legitimation of her portray him as a more knowledgeable, and thus more powerful person than the biblical Eli. The effect of these changes is to strengthen Eli's stature by eliminating negative aspects of the biblical portrayal and intensifying his positive qualities and his divinely protected position of leadership in the community.

Pseudo-Philo adds the people as characters, both in episode one, where they request a leader, and in episode four, where they bring Samuel to Eli, anoint him and bless him. Although they are not strongly defined as characters, their role in the narrative serves to highlight the public plot, diminish Hannah's person and role, and strengthen Eli's stature in the community.

Elkanah has a larger role early in the narrative, but he drops out of the story earlier than in the biblical account. In episode one he declines the position of leader that falls to him when lots are cast. In episode two he consoles Hannah with his four questions, but then he disappears from the narrative. There is no mention that he fathers the child or that he discusses with Hannah the timing of Samuel's dedication. The result of these changes, like others, is complex. They strengthen his position of leadership early in the narrative. But his unwillingness to accept the leadership role is portrayed as an unfaithful act, as a result of which he fades out of the story. This diminishment of Elkanah occurs at the same time as the strengthening of Eli in the story, in keeping with *Pseudo-Philo's* tendency to portray faithful leaders in a strong light.

Several contrasts emerge through the characterization. Hannah's diminished personal stature contrasts with Eli's increased status. Elkanah's early disappearance contrasts with the people's continuing presence and activity at both the beginning and the end of the narrative. Peninnah's taunts serve to strengthen the portrayal of Hannah's desperation, thus further underscoring her diminished personal stature. But on the other hand, *Biblical Antiquities* contrasts the diminished aspects of Hannah with her stronger dimension.[38] For *Pseudo-Philo*, Hannah plays a significant role in the transition to monarchy. She nourishes not only her son Samuel but also the 12 tribes. She utters her testament on the occasion of Eli's official recognition of the boy Samuel, who fulfills the divine promise, and of her whose milk will nourish the people. In this light, Hannah's testament becomes the transitional vehicle by which leadership passes to her son Samuel.

As a result, in contrast with 1 Samuel, in which she is the mother of Samuel the priest, prophet and kingmaker, in *Biblical Antiquities* she is mother of the 'light to the peoples' (51.6), whose milk nourishes with wisdom her son and all people. Motherhood takes on new meaning as the means of passing wisdom to the next generation. She teaches by addressing all nations and kingdoms (51.3), and by expanding the biblical verse 'It is YHWH who puts to death and restores to life, who banishes to Sheol and raises up' (1 Sam. 2.6) into a lesson about eschatology.

In other words, Hannah rests within the Hebrew tradition by which

---

38. P. van der Horst discusses the same tension with regard to Job's first wife Sitis in *T. Job*, and contrasts it with the situation of the daughters of his second wife Dinah; 'Images of Women in the Testament of Job', in M.A. Knibb and P.W. van der Horst (eds.), *Studies on the Testament of Job* (SNTSMS, 66; Cambridge: Cambridge University Press, 1969), pp. 96-106.

women are validated by motherhood, but that validation becomes her own transition to teacher of wisdom, the path to life after death.

Hannah and the Love Motif

Another puzzling aspect of the story is the absence of the love motif in respect to Hannah. The motif appears in the biblical narrative at several points. It states that Elkanah gave 'Hannah a double portion, because he loved her' (1 Sam. 1.5),[39] and records Elkanah's question to her, 'Am I not more to you than ten sons?' (1.8). In *Biblical Antiquities* the motif plays a more prominent part. In episode one God promises to love Samuel as Isaac was loved. In episode two, Peninnah taunts Hannah with the love motif. Later in the narrative, God considers how to call Samuel and observes, 'Behold now Samuel is young so as to be beloved before me' (53.2).

But when Hannah asks for a child, she expresses concern not for love but about wealth: 'I know that neither she who has many sons is rich nor she who has few is poor, but whoever abounds in the will of God is rich' (50.5). And *Biblical Antiquities* does not mention Elkanah's love for Hannah, eliminating any mention of the problematic double portion (perhaps precisely because it is problematic). And his four questions do not include any reference to his love for her.[40] Thus the motif itself is stronger in *Biblical Antiquities* than in 1 Samuel, but it is absent from Hannah's concerns and from Elkanah's feelings for her. This absence seems to set her apart from the usual concerns of the people, on one hand putting her on a pedestal above them, but on the other marginalizing her by making her different.

Two Plots into One

The shifts in characterization call attention to the moment in the plot when the public and private merge. Hannah was transformed from a God-fearing but timid and insecure person to a teacher of wisdom when Eli announced that she was mother of all Israel. Eli could have made the announcement much sooner in the narrative. But he withheld from her the information about the public promise of a son until after the private promise was fulfilled. Then he made known that the private promise was merely at the service of the public one. Samuel was providentially an answer to Hannah's prayers but he had already been

---

39. But see NRSV textual note.
40. But see n. 13 above.

promised as the new leader and prophet.

As soon as Hannah learned from Eli that she had become the mother of the 12 tribes, she broke into song. She had taken Samuel to Shiloh to present him to Eli. But since she had not promised him to the Lord, as she had in the biblical account, there was no question of fulfilling a vow. Instead, she sang in response to Eli's announcement that, as Samuel's mother, she would nourish the 12 tribes.

Looking at plot and characters in this way highlights certain dimensions of the narrative. First, Hannah is both diminished and expanded in various ways from the biblical personage. These contrasting shifts, while problematic from the perspective of narrative unity, are consistent with the overall project in *Biblical Antiquities*, that is to highlight divine guidance of the people and particularly their leaders and to instruct about eschatology. Second, as a result of the expansions she marks the transition to a new era of leadership in giving birth to Samuel and teaching the people about the larger meaning of life. Her teaching takes the form of a testament, a form used by leaders in times of transition. It is presented in public, at the shrine at Shiloh. But it marks the passing of leadership not from her or from Elkanah to their son, but from God to their son at the people's request, and Hannah serves as the human mouthpiece that expresses this transferral of leadership. Third, Hannah assumes the role of wisdom teacher, thus expanding the role of motherhood to include transmitting lessons of life to the next generation.[41]

---

41. Divine action in the events of history is a prominent theme throughout *Biblical Antiquities* See F.J. Murphy, 'God in Pseudo-Philo', *JJS* 19 (1988), pp. 1-18.

Chapter 4

THE SONG OF HANNAH IN *TARGUM OF THE PROPHETS*

The Hannah narrative in *Targum of the Prophets* (*Targ. Neb.*) is identical to the biblical story, but the Song of Hannah is altered and expanded dramatically. This chapter will therefore focus only on the Song, its background, literary features and themes.

Introductory Topics

A few general remarks about the Targum will situate the Song in its literary context. *Targum of the Prophets* was most likely composed in Judea over a period of centuries beginning around 135 CE in Palestine. Quite possibly, later editors working in Babylonia inserted additional material into the text. But the Song could well have been interpreted and inserted independently, either before or during that period. Daniel Harrington sets its date of composition between 70 CE and the fall of the Roman Empire.[1] The translation into Aramaic follows the biblical Masoretic text fairly literally for the most part, but a few poetic passages consist of free, midrashic paraphrase.[2] In the books of Samuel these include the Song of Hannah in 1 Samuel 2 and David's words in 2 Samuel 22.1–23.7.

Like all the Targums, it translates and expands the Hebrew Bible in order to interpret it for a postexilic synagogue community. Typical of contemporaneous writings it avoids anthropomorphisms when speaking

1. D.J. Harrington, 'The Apocalypse of Hannah: Targum Jonathan of 1 Samuel 2:1-10', in D.M. Golomb (ed.), *'Working With No Data': Semitic and Egyptian Studies Presented to Thomas O. Lambdin* (Winona Lake, IN: Eisenbrauns, 1987), pp. 147-52; D.J. Harrington and A.J. Saldarini, *Targum Jonathan of the Former Prophets: Introduction, Translation and Notes* (The Aramaic Bible, 10; Wilmington, DE: Michael Glazier, 1987), p. 3.
2. J. Neusner, *What Is Midrash?* (Philadelphia: Fortress Press, 1987), p. 7.

of God, emphasizes respect for Israel and its elders, and explains or smooths over difficult or contradictory texts to make the Bible accessible to the audience at weekly synagogue services.[3]

The Targumic Song of Hannah

The Song of Hannah in this targum is remarkable because of the extensive additions it contains, in contrast to the absence of significant changes elsewhere in *Targum of the Prophets* I will analyze the Song with particular attention to the additions and the shifts in emphasis they create.

The targumic Song clearly takes the biblical poem as its point of departure. To illustrate, the biblical words are italicized in the following translation from ch. 2.[4]

> 1. *And Hannah prayed* in a spirit of prophecy *and said*: 'Now Samuel my son is to be a prophet on behalf of Israel. In his days they will be saved from the hand of the Philistines, and by his hands signs and mighty deeds will be done for them. Therefore *my heart* is strong in the portion that *the Lord* has given to me. And also Heman, the son of Joel, the son of my son Samuel who is to arise—he and his fourteen sons are to be speaking in song by means of lyres and lutes with their brothers the Levites to give praise in the house of the sanctuary. Therefore *my horn is exalted* in the gift that *the Lord* has appointed for me. And also concerning the marvelous revenge that will be against the Philistines who are to bring the ark on a new cart, and with it the guilt offering. Therefore the assembly of Israel will say: "*Let my mouth* be open to speak great things *against my enemies, for I rejoice in your saving power.*"' 2. Concerning Sennacherib the king of Assyria—she prophesied and said that he and all his armies would come up against Jerusalem, and a great sign would be worked on him; there the corpses of his camp would fall. Therefore all the nations, peoples, and language groups will confess and say: '*There is not one* who is holy except *the Lord, for there is no one apart from you*'; and your people will say: '*There is no one* who is strong except *our God.*' 3. Concerning Nebuchadnezzar the king of Babylon—she prophesied and said: 'You Chaldeans and all the peoples who are to rule in Israel, do not say many boastful things. *Let not* blasphemies *go forth from your mouth*, for the all-knowing *God is the Lord* and upon all his works he fixes judgment. And also to you he is to repay the revenge of your sins.' 4. Concerning the kingdoms of Greece—she prophesied and said: '*The bows of the* Greek *warriors will be broken*; and those of the

---

3.   McNamara, *Targum*, pp. 31-34, 69-78.
4.   Harrington and Saldarini, *Targum*, pp. 105-106.

house of the Hasmonean who were weak—mighty deeds will be done for them.' 5. Concerning the sons of Haman—she prophesied and said: 'Those who were *filled up on bread* and growing in wealth and abounding in money have become poor; they have returned to working as laborers for bread, the food of their mouth. Mordecai and Esther who were needy became rich and forgot their poverty; they returned to being free persons. So Jerusalem, which was like *a barren woman*, is to be filled with her exiled people. And Rome, which was filled with great numbers of people—her armies will cease to be; she will be desolate and destroyed. 6. All these are the mighty works *of the Lord*, who is powerful in the world. *He puts to death* and speaks so as to make alive; *he brings down to Sheol*, and he is also ready *to bring up* in eternal life. 7. *The Lord makes poor and makes rich; he humbles, also he exalts.* 8. *He raises up the poor from the dust, from the dunghill he exalts the needy one*, to make them dwell *with* the righteous ones, *the chiefs* of the world; and he bequeaths to them *thrones of glory*, for before the Lord the deeds of the sons of men are revealed. He has established Gehenna below for the wicked ones. And the just ones—those doing his good pleasure, he has established the world for them. 9. *He will keep* away from Gehenna the bodies of his servants, the righteous ones. And *the wicked ones* will walk about in Gehenna *in the darkness*, to make it known that there is no one in whom there is strength having claim for the day of judgment. 10. *The Lord will shatter the enemies* who rise up to do harm to his people. The Lord blasts down *upon them* from *the heavens* with a loud voice. He will exact just revenge from God and the army of the violent nations who come with him from *the ends of the earth. And he will give power to his king and will magnify* the kingdom of *his anointed one.*'

Analysis of the Song

The changes in the words of the Song shift its genre from hymn to apocalypse. The Song expresses two different temporal modes that divide the Song into two parts, vv. 1-5 and 6-10. The first part is about twice as long as the second. The first foretells specific periods and events in Israel's history and the second predicts and describes the final judgment and its consequences. Thematically the expanded poem particularizes and broadens the scope of divine dominion. Geographically it expands to include both Israel and Gehenna, and temporally it broadens to encompass both this life and the next. I will analyze both sections below.

The first five verses contain retrospective predictions about the history of Israel: divine intervention ensures major military victories against the Philistines, Sennacherib, Nebuchadnezzar, Greece, Haman and Rome. The second half of the Song teaches about divine eschato-logical activity: the Lord reverses economic and moral fortunes in the present and future; and highlights the content and artistry of the composition.

The first half has three parts: Hannah's words of praise in v. 1a, her report of others' praise in vv. 1b-2, and her report of divine actions on behalf of Israel against its enemies in vv. 3-5.

The introductory half-verse identifies Hannah's mode of speaking as prophetic. Throughout the rest of the Song it becomes clear that 'prophecy' here means 'prediction', in which Hannah foretells events in Israel's history. She then refers to her son as a prophet. In his case the word seems to mean 'judge', according to the actions Hannah names: he will save the people from the Philistines, in the manner of the biblical judges. She further emphasizes his importance to the community by naming three generations of his descendants and associating them with the Levites who would serve as musicians in the sanctuary (v. 1). The official roles are specified in this declaration, which is given in parallel form, first about Samuel and then about his grandson Heman and his 14 sons. Hannah predicts the deeds of each, then praises God for those deeds. The catchword בכן (therefore) that appears twice in the verse highlights the parallel structure introducing Hannah's words of praise, which she sings as a result of the deeds of Samuel and his descendants. Verses 1b-5 pick up the thread introduced by the word 'Philistines', and make predictions about the five major enemies of ancient Israel in chronological order: Philistines, Sennacherib, Nebuchadnezzar, Greece, Haman and Rome.

The section has a complex structure. Verses 1b and 2 overlap in structure with v. 1b and vv. 3-5. Like 1a, they predict actions, then announce consequent praise to God. Like vv. 3-5, they begin with על (concerning), followed by a particular enemy of the Israelites and mention of that enemy's actions. Verse 1b has a further similarity with 1a insofar as it continues the quotation of Hannah's words from the beginning of the Song. But v. 2 changes that pattern by placing the introductory phrase, 'concerning...' in the mouth of the narrator rather than Hannah. In vv. 1-2 the 'therefore' parts of the utterance retain the biblical words. But in vv. 3-5, the biblical words are applied to the different enemies and what will befall them.

In a further similarity to v. 1a, vv. 1b-2 repeat the catchword בכין to introduce praise to God. The first two times, Hannah names her own response to the Lord's gifts that will come through Samuel and his grandson and 14 great-grandsons. The last three times, she names the response of others: 'the assembly of Israel', 'all nations, peoples, and language groups', and finally 'your people'.

Overlapping structures continue in vv. 2-5a with the catchphrase אתנביאת ואמרת (she prophesied and said). This phrase is condensed from the opening statement of the Song, וצליאתח חנה בברות אתנביאת ואמרת (Hannah prayed in a spirit of prophecy and said). It introduces either the actions of the enemy or the punishment each in turn will suffer.

At the end of v. 1 the words of the assembly of Israel form an inclusion with a reference to the Lord in v. 10. The assembly says, 'Let my mouth be open to speak great things against my enemies...' and in v. 10 'the Lord blasts down upon them from the heavens with a loud voice'. The inclusion expresses the dual themes of the Song: praise of God and condemnation of enemies, and further unifies the whole.

Verses 4 and 5 follow the pattern of reversals in the biblical Song: vv. 4 and 5a begin with the fate of the enemy, contrasting it with that of Israel. Verse 5b begins with Jerusalem, then names the fate of Rome. This pattern of editing the biblical Song with additions, catchwords and phrases and reversals unifies the first half of the targumic Song under the theme of divine intervention in Israel's history. Each episode is described as a prediction with the exception of the fifth, which comments on the past situation of Mordecai, Esther and the sons of Haman. The five appearances of 'prophecy' or 'prophesy' highlight the predictive quality of Hannah's words, retrospectively assuring Israel from the time of Samuel that God will intervene on its behalf throughout history.

The second half of the Song moves to a different temporal mode, the eschatological, and the literary features support that emphasis. Three parts can be identified: the transition in v. 6a, a list of divine apocalyptic deeds (vv. 6b-9), and a description of the definitive apocalyptic moment in v. 10. The literary features in vv. 6-10 are less easily defined than those in the first half, because they do not fall into as neat a pattern. When Hannah predicts the future according to real time, she speaks with less clarity and precision than when she speaks from the benefit of hindsight. But vv. 6-10 coincide more strongly with the biblical Song than do the first five verses. A careful look at the second half of the Song illustrates that feature.

Verse 6 begins with a transition, in which the phrase כלאאלין (all these) refers back to the historical section and forward to the eschatological. At the same time it specifies the world as the locus of divine activity and intention in both temporal modes. The rest of the Song follows the basic structure of the biblical Song, with its antithetical pairs, several of which are further elaborated by relevant comments. But the minor variations in wording camouflage the dramatic shift in content of vv. 6-10 to describe divine eschatological intervention.

Verse 6 changes the biblical מחיה (restores to life) to אמר לאחאה (speaks so as to make alive) focusing on the power of the divine word. The following stich substitutes for יעל (raises up) the programmatic עתיד לאסקא בחיי עלמא (is ready to bring up in eternal life) introducing the eschatological theme. Verses 7 and 8a follow the biblical Song exactly. Verse 8b specifies that the biblical nobles are the righteous ones, then names the rationale for divine activity: קדם יוי גלן עובדי בני אנשא מלרע (for before the Lord the deeds of the sons of men are revealed). The Song elaborates at this point on the eschatological plan, which broadens the spatial limits of divine activity beyond earth to Gehenna[5] just as the temporal has expanded beyond history to eternal life. The section designates earth as the territory of the righteous, who will continue a bodily existence, as will the wicked who are condemned to walk about in Gehenna. The assignment of people to reward or punishment will take place on the day of judgment.

Verse 10 emphasizes the divine victory over the enemy by using the active voice. Then it reiterates the emphasis on God's voice from v. 6, making a parallel to the biblical ירום (thunders) with עליהון מן שמיא בקל רם ישקיף יוי (blasts down upon them with a loud voice) and stressing the punitive power of the divine word and completing the inclusion from v. 1. In addition it provides closure in summarizing both parts of the Song, the historical and the eschatological, by naming the people's enemies in general and the apocalyptic God in particular. The allusion to God (see Ezek. 38–39) alludes to the apocalyptic tone of the great eschatological battle in which God will emerge as victor. In this apocalyptic context, the anointed one whose kingdom God will magnify is an eschatological messiah.[6]

5. Harrington, 'Apocalypse of Hannah', p. 151.
6. Harrington and Saldarini, *Targum*, p. 106 n. 10.

Targumic Changes to the Biblical Song

This analysis of the targumic Song illustrates several types of changes it makes to the biblical Song. Several of these are relatively simple and straightforward; for example, in a few instances the Targum substitutes adjectives for nouns or concepts for symbols, retaining the biblical meaning of the phrase. The biblical 'there is no Rock like our God' in v. 2 becomes 'There is no one who is strong except our God.' In v. 3 the biblical 'for the Lord is a God of knowledge' becomes in the Targum 'for the all-knowing God is the Lord'. The biblical 'the Most High will thunder in heaven' becomes 'The Lord blasts down upon them from the heavens with a loud voice' in v. 10. In v. 9 the biblical 'feet' of those in Gehenna becomes 'bodies', thus eliminating the synecdoche. The example from v. 10 illustrates a shift toward more cumbersome wording, but a different example shows a paraphrase from more to less awkward: 'Talk no more so very proudly, let not arrogance come from your mouth' in the biblical versions becomes the targumic 'Let not blasphemies go forth from your mouth' (v. 3).

Several simple substitutions and additions have theological implications. For example, v. 6 adds the verb 'speaks', changing the kind of divine intervention from action to word. And v. 9 substitutes 'righteous' for 'faithful', specifying the nature of fidelity.

In some instances lengthy additions particularize the meaning of indefinite or general nouns or phrases. This type of expansion dramatically affects the meaning of the Song and divides it into two thematic units, vv. 1-5 and 7-10, with v. 1 introducing the whole and v. 6 forming the transition between them.

Verse 1 adds 'in a spirit of prophecy' to the biblical 'and Hannah prayed', setting the tone for the predictive additions that follow. It further elaborates, 'Now Samuel my son is to be a prophet on behalf of Israel.' The Song thus announces Samuel's future role and provides the reason why Hannah sings at his dedication. The addition 'And also Heman, the son of Joel, the son of my son Samuel who is to arise—he and his 14 sons are to be speaking in song by means of lyres and lutes with their brothers the Levites to give praise in the house of the sanctuary' provides further detail about Samuel's descendants (see 1 Chron. 6.33; 15.16-17; 25.4-8; 2 Chron. 5.12-13).

The biblical Song uses the word 'enemies' in v. 1; in vv. 1-5 the targumic version inserts references to the Philistines, Sennacherib the king of Assyria, Nebuchadnezzar the king of Babylon, the kingdoms of

Greece and the sons of Haman, Mordecai and Esther, and Rome. It adds specific details about the enmity of each toward Israel, describing them in future terms: the Philistines would 'bring the ark on a new cart, and with it the guilt offering'; Sennacherib's armies 'would come up against Jerusalem, and a great sign would be worked on him; there the corpses of his camp would fall'. Nebuchadnezzar would 'rule in Israel'; among the kingdoms of Greece the Song refers to 'the house of the Hasmonean who were weak'.

In vv. 1-4 the Targum then uses the biblical words to foretell the consequences that would befall the enemies. In v. 1 the biblical words are spoken by the assembly of Israel against the Philistines. Verse 2 puts the biblical words in the mouths of 'all the nations, peoples, and language groups' who praise God for destroying the Assyrian armies (see Dan. 3.4). Verse 3 uses the biblical words to admonish the Babylonians. The biblical words in v. 4 predict the defeat of the Greeks, and in v. 5 they describe conditions before the enemy's defeat: the sons of Haman were 'filled up on bread' while Jerusalem 'was like a barren woman'. These expansions create a prediction by Hannah of divine protection of Israel throughout the ages of its history.[7] The transitional v. 6 in the targumic version first summarizes vv. 1-5, then adds the words 'ready' and 'eternal' in the second half: 'He is also ready to bring up in eternal life.' These simple words actually shift the temporal focus of the second half of the Song from time to eternity. They then develop the apocalyptic allusion introduced in the first half by the references to the ages in Israel's history. Further additions describe the final judgment, the terms by which all will be judged, and the eternal consequences of reward and punishment.

In v. 8 the biblical 'sit with princes and inherit a seat of honor' expands to 'dwell with the righteous ones, the chiefs of the world; and he reserves for them thrones of glory, for before the Lord the deeds of the sons of men are revealed. He has established Gehenna below for the wicked ones. And the just ones—those doing his good pleasure, he has established the world for them.' The expansion identifies the biblical 'princes' as the 'righteous ones'. It then specifies that the biblical 'seat of honor' is the 'thrones of glory', the world, the place of reward for the just, who follow the divine will. The expansion broadens the spatial

---

7. Several centuries later, *Gen. Rab.* 44.17 recounts that Abraham foresaw the monarchies of Babylonia, Media, Greece and Edom (Rome). See Neusner, *What Is Midrash?*, p. 62.

realm beyond the biblical earthly world, specifying that Gehenna is made for the wicked.

Verse 9 further develops the eschatological theme by expanding the biblical words to develop the topics of Gehenna and the day of judgment. It alludes to the eliminated 'feet', specifying that 'the wicked ones will walk about in Gehenna, in the darkness'. The biblical darkness is thus given a specific location. And the expansions focus on Gehenna to contrast the righteous and the wicked. The targumic version reads, 'He will keep away from Gehenna the bodies of his servants, the righteous ones' before stating that the wicked will walk in it. By locating the action in relation to Gehenna the targumic version reinforces the shift from this life to the next. It continues in that vein by stating the divine purpose, 'to make it known that there is no one in whom there is strength having claim for the day of judgment'. The expansion affirms the futility of personal strength or self-sufficiency. And it specifies the moment of reckoning as the 'day of judgment'.

Verse 10 elaborates on that decisive moment. It first identifies the biblical divine enemies as those 'who rise up to do harm to his people'. Verses 1-5 name the enemies in six ages of Israel; here the Targum refers to 'Gog and the army of the violent nations who come with him from the ends of the earth'. Rather than the burial announced in Ezek. 39.11-16 for the apocalyptic foe, the targumic version declares simply, 'He will exact just revenge from God.'[8]

Characterization in the Targumic Song
The formal characteristics of the Song support the characterization of Hannah, God and Samuel. Hannah herself expands from the faithful woman who rejoices in her motherhood to prophet who predicts the divine military might and judgment. She joins the ranks of the women who sing victory hymns, but differs from Miriam and Deborah in predicting divine success rather than celebrating the accomplished facts. The targumic Hannah assumes in addition the position of teacher by articulating the eschatological belief the Song contains. In this respect she serves in a capacity similar to Hannah in *Pseudo-Philo*'s *Biblical Antiquities*. That woman also teaches about life after death, but offers

---

8.   Targumic translation techniques are discussed in Harrington and Saldarini, *Targum*, pp. 4-13. In some instances they differ from those that occur in the targumic 1 Sam. 2.1-10 and 2 Sam. 22–23, suggesting multiple authorship of the targums.

the lesson explicitly from her position as mother. Here Hannah speaks more as a predictor of the eschaton in the spirit of prophecy in which she sings her Song. Hannah serves a function in the Song, as well as in the surrounding narrative, as a bridge between two times. Earlier we saw that the Song divides in half temporally. In fact Hannah stands in time between the two temporal modes: she speaks in the Targum after the completion of her historical predictions, with the exception of the fate of Rome. But the eschatological event has not yet taken place in her Song or in the course of events. Likewise Hannah bridges two times in Israel's history: the period of the judges and the formation of the monarchy. In this respect the form of the Song supports the characterization of the singer.

Absent from the Song is any allusion to barren mothers as individuals. Instead, the Targum uses the biblical phrase to symbolize Jerusalem repopulated with returning exiles (see Isa. 54.1-3). The image here refers to Hellenistic times rather than Persian, and adapts the biblical use of names of cities as daughters such as in Isa. 10.32.

In contrast, Samuel, whose birth and dedication offer the occasion for singing the Song, appears here in only a minor role. His mother proclaims his future as prophet and predicts that he will accomplish great things for Israel. Then he recedes entirely, and the Song moves quickly to the generations of his descendants and the centuries beyond his lifetime.

The targumic Song's depiction of God as victorious warrior reflects the period of the Judges at the end of which Hannah appears. In fact the targumic Song emphasizes this divine quality to a far greater extent than does the biblical Song. Here Hannah projects the warrior image forward throughout the ensuing millennium, as she predicts the downfall of the Philistines, Sennacherib, Nebuchadnezzar, Greece, Haman and Rome; each the result of divine mighty works in the world. And Hannah likewise predicts the divine victory in the apocalyptic battle against God and his armies from the ends of the earth.

In fact in this respect the targumic Song calls to mind the biblical Miriam's words 'Sing to the Lord, who has triumphed gloriously; Horse and rider have been thrown into the sea' (Exod. 15.21) celebrating the defeat of Pharaoh's army, and Deborah's Song, 'Lord, when you went out from Seir, when you marched from the region of Edom...the mountains quaked before the Lord, the One of Sinai, before the Lord the God of Israel' (Judg. 5.4a, 5).

The biblical Hannah's 'My mouth derides my enemies because I rejoice in your victory' (1 Sam. 2.1) appears vague and almost timid in contrast to the targumic elaboration.

Besides emphasizing the divine warrior, the Targum calls attention to God as judge. In v. 3 Hannah sings, 'for the all-knowing God is the Lord and upon all his works he fixes judgment'. Then in the eschatological section she asserts that all human deeds will be revealed to the Lord, who will set the righteous on thrones of glory and banish the evil to Gehenna (v. 8), again a more intense assertion than the biblical 'by God actions are weighed' (v. 3).

Theological Themes

The Song's form and characterization express the theological themes of divine intervention and eschatology. In the first part Hannah predicts that the Deity will guide Israel to victory and its enemies to defeat at each major juncture in its military and political history. These forecasts of success support the belief in God's unconditional election and protection of Israel from the time of the divine covenant with David (2 Sam. 7.15-16).[9] To be sure, the Song benefits from hindsight and enables the singer to assure the listener of divine reliability, power and concern throughout the exigencies of Israel's history to date. The implicit conviction carries the more weight for the listener because the historical evidence favors Israel in each episode that Hannah predicts. In this way history becomes the reason why Israel can count on divine intervention in the future that Hannah's listeners face in real time.

The second half of the Song moves to eschatological time with the mention of eternal life, expressing ideas foreign to the time of Hannah and Samuel but of urgent concern at the turn of the era. Eschatological time involves the time after the final judgment, but considers that time in a linear progression with time as we know it in this life. Thus two temporal modalities telescope into one, providing continuity with the existing notion of time as well as adding a new temporal modality. The same is true of the Song's notion of place. Sheol is identified by inference as the place of punishment, in contrast not to a place but to eternal life (v. 6). Then the place of punishment is named as Gehenna, which is established for the wicked, a dark place where the wicked will walk about. But the place of reward is the world, where those to be rewarded

9.   Cf. the Mosaic injunction that blessing will reward obedience, but disobedience will be punished, e.g., Deut. 11.22-31.

will receive thrones of glory. This delineation of space provides continuity of place for the righteous, while requiring the evil ones to move to a different location. This manipulation of time and place emphasizes continuity in both spheres, particularly for those to be rewarded. There is no special, new place of reward to which the righteous will go at a particular moment in time or after time. As a result, the banishment of the evil to Sheol or Gehenna takes on the quality of punishment not only because of the nature of that particular place but also by very reason of the fact that it is a different place which can be reached only by leaving behind this world. By contrast, part of the reward for the righteous is the opportunity to remain in this world. Such a notion reflects an implicit belief in the goodness of this world.

The Song articulates various details about reward and punishment. In the first place, they depend on people's deeds. Verse 8 specifies that those to be rewarded are the poor and needy, the righteous ones (who are the chiefs of the world) and the just (who follow the divine pleasure). God will keep the righteous away from Gehenna. Those to be punished are the wicked, those who rely on their own strength (v. 9). The nature of the reward and punishment is directly tied into the telescoped times and places discussed above: the reward will be eternal life, and the punishment will be to walk about in the darkness of Gehenna (vv. 6, 8, 9). Such a punishment seems to suggest that those to be punished will not be in the temporal mode of eternity, but will remain in time as it is now known. However, those who will remain in the familiar place will be the rewarded ones. Hence, while this world is seen as good, the present time appears less ideal.

The time for meting out reward and punishment will be the day of judgment. The actual act of passage from the present life to reward or punishment remains unspecified, but the Song's parallel antitheses in v. 6—'puts to death and speaks so as to make alive' and 'brings down to Sheol, and is ready to bring up in eternal life'—imply that death marks the passage to reward or punishment. The Song offers no clear statement of any difference between personal death and the day of judgment; hence there is no two-step judgment such as Christianity today knows as particular and general judgment. One can only speculate as to whether this represents another telescoping of time or simply a detail that was not included in the Song.

Finally, these aspects of reward and punishment seem to suggest that all will retain bodily existence. Those in Gehenna will walk about, and those in the world will have thrones. If bodily form will change in any way, the Song does not so indicate.

A final aspect of the teaching about reward and punishment after death follows from the placement of vv. 6-10 after 1-5. The first half of the Song has specified that divine intervention on Israel's behalf can be counted on. Since the Song delivers this message from the perspective of hindsight, it assumes the same weight as Israel's frequent recitals of divine guidance throughout history from the time of the Exodus: that is, it functions as a reason to believe that God will continue to protect the chosen people. In this context, divine protection extends beyond the present existence into the eternal mode that the second half of the Song describes. But Hannah's predictions about Israel's immediate future serve more imminently to offer assurance that rewards and punishments are meted out not only in the final analysis but in every age. Israel's enemies will suffer defeat at every juncture through the divine intervention that will assure Israel's success. In fact, in keeping with the Davidic covenant, Hannah foretells that victories depend exclusively on divine intervention, and not at all on human effort (v. 9; 2 Sam. 7.15-16).

The Targum's Apocalyptic Community

The theological themes of the Song raise a question about the nature of the Jewish community who produced the targumic Song of Hannah. Their concerns about the historical and eschatological future are expressed in predictions about military encounters in which the divine warrior triumphs and the divine judge decides the consequences for nations and individuals. The question of what will happen after and as a result of the specific events in Israel's history is considered in apocalyptic terms; and questions about the nature of the end time loom large. This manner of expression is associated in biblical and later writings with communities who perceive their situation as uncertain and vulnerable in the face of immense threats to their very existence. It challenges those threats with its implicit exhortation to trust that 'the integrity of values can be maintained in the face of social and political powerlessness and even the threat of death'.[10] This hope, born of a steadfast belief

---

10. J.J. Collins, *The Apocalyptic Imagination: An Introduction to the Jewish Matrix of Christianity* (New York: Crossroad, 1984), p. 215.

in divine intervention on the people's behalf, is the hallmark of the community in question.

Just as with *Pseudo-Philo*'s *Biblical Antiquities*, the significant additions and interpretive reworkings of the biblical Song invite us to consider the implications of its being sung by a woman. Did women have a public place in community and synagogue? Did the community look to women as teachers? as prophets? Were women authors? Might a woman have composed this expanded version of the biblical Song? And if so, does the prominent position the Song ascribes to Hannah represent not the reality of the community's customs but rather the hopes of individuals within it? Or does the targumic community identify the female singer as Israel, personified by Isaiah as the barren one who bore many children, peopling the desolate cities after the exile (Isa. 54.1-3)? These speculations invite further study.

The divine guidance throughout Israel's past and present which the Song affirms, and in the future for which the Song expresses hope, suggest its provenance within a community ravaged by destruction and demoralization. Such a group would have reason to look back on its history and affirm God's protection throughout, in the hope that divine guidance on their behalf would extend to their immediate and long-term future.

In its historical context the expanded Song reminds the reader of the Lord's continuing protection of the community during the most vulnerable episodes of its past. And it offers an eternal reward as a reason to remain faithful during a period when temporal reasons were scarce.

Chapter 5

LUKE'S INFANCY NARRATIVE

Analysis of Luke's Infancy Narrative in light of the Hannah story in 1 Samuel can be compared to looking into a kaleidoscope at brightly colored chips arranged in an elaborate pattern, formed by rotating the lens slightly to disarrange an elegantly simple one. The new formation offers a different type of beauty: stunning arrangement of details into a complex whole. The shift in the kaleidoscopic image from simple to complex offers in metaphorical form a description of the shift in language, motifs and theme from 1 Samuel's to Luke's Infancy Narrative (chs. 1–2). In this chapter I will analyze that elaborate variation on the Hannah story.

Provenance of Luke's Work

The two-volume work known as Luke–Acts was most likely composed for a Hellenistic, urban, Gentile-Christian community in the years following the destruction of the Temple (c. 80–95 CE). The author's reliance on Mark's Gospel and on 'Q' and 'L' sources for the work is widely recognized. The geographic location of the community for whom the work was written is unknown, but was probably Christianized during a mission of Paul to Antioch. The hymns most likely circulated independently before they were included in the narrative.[1]

---

1. R.E. Brown, *The Birth of the Messiah: A Commentary on the Infancy Narratives in Matthew and Luke* (Garden City, NY: Doubleday, 1977); J.A. Fitzmyer, *The Gospel According to Luke I–IX: Introduction, Translation, and Notes* (AB, 28; Garden City, NY: Doubleday, 1981), pp. 35-97; L.T. Johnson, *The Gospel of Luke* (Sacra Pagina; Collegeville, MN: Liturgical Press, 1991), pp. 2-10; B.E. Reid, *Choosing the Better Part? Women in the Gospel of Luke* (Collegeville, MN: Liturgical Press, 1996), pp. 17-18, 75.

Canonical Contexts

As is the case with the Hannah narrative in 1 Samuel, Luke's Infancy Narrative is situated in different contexts with their own particular meanings. The narrative can be read as the introduction to Luke–Acts, in which case it introduces the coming of Jesus within the context of the history of Israel. Chapters 1–2 describe the circumstances of Jesus' birth, the rest of the Gospel relates Jesus' life among the people and their rejection of his teaching, and Acts recounts the efforts of his witnesses to offer the teachings to a broader audience. The widening circles of followers of Jesus could find in the account assurance that their beliefs and practices were rooted in the time of Jesus.[2] Johnson observes the similarity between this structure and the Pentateuch's story of Moses.[3]

The second context of Luke's Infancy Narrative is the gospel apart from Acts. Within that framework the first two chapters introduce the account of the life and teachings of Jesus without including the widening of his influence.

A third context within which to read the Lukan account is in relation to Matthew 1–2, the only other Gospel account of Jesus' birth. Both stories include several details: Jesus' birth is situated in relation to the reign of Herod (Lk. 1.5; Mt. 2.1); Mary his mother is a virgin betrothed to Joseph (Lk. 1.27, 34; Mt. 1.16, 20); Joseph belongs to the house of David (Lk. 1.27; 2.4; Mt. 1.16, 20); an angel announces Jesus' birth (Lk. 1.28-30; Mt. 1.20-21); Jesus is recognized as a son of David (Lk. 1.32; Mt. 1.1); the Holy Spirit, but not Joseph, will be involved in his conception (Lk. 1.34-35; Mt. 1.18-25); Jesus' name is announced by the angel, as is his title 'Savior' (Lk. 1.31; 2.11; Mt. 1.21); the birth takes place in Bethlehem after Mary and Joseph's wedding (Lk. 2.4-7; Mt. 1.24-25; 2.1); the family live in Nazareth (Lk. 2.39; Mt. 2.22-23). But they contain significant differences as well. Matthew alone mentions the magi and all the events related to them: the star, Herod's plot, the killing of the children, and the family's flight to Egypt. On the other hand, Luke alone includes information about Zechariah, Elizabeth and John; Mary and Joseph's trip to Bethlehem for the census, the visit by the shepherds, the presentation of Jesus in the Temple, and the incident

---

2.   Fitzmyer, *Luke*, pp. 9-10.
3.   Johnson, *Luke*, pp. 19-21.

at the Temple when Jesus was 12 years old. It also includes the Songs sung by Zechariah, Mary and Simeon and mentions the prophetess Anna. These differences support the distinct messages of the two evangelists.[4]

Each of the three contexts puts the Infancy Narrative in a unique perspective. The first highlights the continuing influence of Jesus and his teachings, the second emphasizes the teaching itself, and the third calls attention to the inclusion of the Gentiles and the rootedness of Jesus' life and teachings in the traditions of Israel.

The Plot of Luke's Infancy Narrative

The complex Lukan narrative interweaves the story of Zechariah, Elizabeth and their son John with that of Mary and her son Jesus. The carefully crafted account highlights the relationships between the two sets of people and events. The connections are evident in the overall structure of the narrative, which can be schematized in a way similar to the Hannah narrative in 1 Samuel. The account has two parallel stories, the first of Zechariah, Elizabeth and John and the second of Mary and Jesus.[5] Each has two movements, simple in the case of Elizabeth and compound in Mary's case. In fact, the Mary movements are about twice as long as the Elizabeth movements, indicating their relative importance in the narrative. The two stories interweave, beginning with both first movements and followed by the two second movements.[6]

The first movement in each story is the announcement and the second the fulfillment of the announcement. Each movement has three parts. The first begins with an introductory statement about the family, followed by an account of events at a strategic location. It climaxes with the words of the mother. The second begins with the birth and naming of the child, including a speech by a significant person. It concludes with a brief summation of his early years and first public appearance.

The story of Zechariah, Elizabeth, and John is introduced in 1.5-7. It then narrates the events in the Temple, when the angel appeared to

---

4. Brown, *Birth*, pp. 34-38; Fitzmyer, *Luke*, p. 307.

5. See the detailed discussions of the two stories in Brown, *Birth*, pp. 248-53, 292-98, 408-10; Fitzmyer, *Luke*, pp. 313-15; R.C. Tannehill, *The Narrative Unity of Luke–Acts: A Literary Interpretation* (Philadelphia: Fortress Press, 1986), pp. 15-44.

6. For an alternative ordering of the narrative see Brown, *Birth*, pp. 248-53.

Zechariah while he was carrying out his priestly duties (vv. 8-23). It climaxes with Elizabeth's words in vv. 24-25. The second movement begins with the mention of John's birth and naming (vv. 57-66). Zechariah's words follow in vv. 67-79, after which John's early years and foreshadowing of his first public appearance are mentioned (v. 80).

The story of Mary and Jesus begins with introductory information in 1.26-27. It then recounts the events in the strategic location, which is Mary's home (vv. 28-38). Mary speaks in v. 38. Then the narrative starts a new first movement, introduced by the news of Mary's trip to the hill country to visit her kinswoman (v. 39). The events in that location, Zechariah and Elizabeth's house, follow in vv. 40-56. The words of both mothers are spoken at that location, in vv. 42-55. The second movement begins with the account of Jesus' birth and naming in 2.1-21. That element compounds with the story of a second ritual, the presentation of Jesus (vv. 22-38). Words are spoken on that occasion by significant people in vv. 28-35 and 38, with an introduction of Anna in vv. 36-37. The second movement ends with an account of Jesus' early years and first public appearance (vv. 39-52).

All four introductory statements include genealogical and biographical information about the families involved. Zechariah is identified as a member of the priestly order of Abijah, and his wife is a descendant of Aaron. The righteousness, blamelessness and age of the couple are noted, as is Elizabeth's barrenness (1.5-7). In Mary's case, she is identified simply as a virgin who lives in Nazareth. Her betrothed is identified as Joseph of the house of David, thus of royal lineage (vv. 26-27). The location of Zechariah and Elizabeth's home is identified in the transitional v. 39, when the narrative tells that Mary hastened to visit her relative in the Judean hill country. Anna is identified as a member of the tribe of Asher and as the daughter of Phanuel. Her seven-year marriage is mentioned, as is her age (84 years). Her lifestyle is also described: she stayed in the Temple and spent her days in prayer and fasting (2.36-37).[7] Several things become apparent in these introductions. Each family has roots in one of the 12 tribes. Elizabeth and Zechariah belong to priestly families, while Joseph's roots are royal. Anna, while not a member of a priestly family, is associated with the Temple. Marital status figures in the introductory information about all

---

7. Note the parallels between Anna and Judith (Jdt. 8.4, 6, 17; 19.1). See Reid, *Better Part*, p. 92.

the people involved, and there are currently no children in any of the families.

The announcements follow in the second parts of the first movement. In Zechariah's case it occurs in the Temple, where he offers the daily sacrifice. It follows the pattern of a call narrative, where a messenger appears and bestows a particular call from God. The recipient objects but the messenger confirms the call in spite of the person's doubts. For Zechariah this means that the angel assures him that his prayers have been heard and his wife will bear a son. We thus learn that Zechariah prayed for a son. When Zechariah questions the angel on account of the ages of himself and his wife, the angel assures him that the birth will occur. Then the sign will be Zechariah's inability to speak until the event takes place (1.8-23).

For Mary, the announcement occurs in her home. She, too, is told of a son to be born to her. And she, too, questions the message since she does not know a man (ἄνδρα οὐ γινώσκω), 1.34. Note the allusion to the observation in 1 Samuel, 'Elkanah knew his wife Hannah'. And the angel reassures her and confirms the promise. The sign of confirmation in her case is the information about Elizabeth's pregnancy.

Part three in both stories is the words of the mother following the announcement of the son to be born. In the case of Zechariah and Elizabeth, the announcement was made to her husband, and we assume that Elizabeth knows nothing about it until she discovers that she is pregnant. We are not told that Zechariah finds a way to give her the news. But when she becomes pregnant, she attributes her good fortune to the Lord, acknowledging the disgrace her barrenness caused her (vv. 24-25). The simple dignity of her words supports the narrative's characterization of her as faithful and righteous. Elizabeth's five-month seclusion seems to explain why Mary is unaware of her relative's condition until Gabriel informs her. Such sequestering is inconsistent with Elizabeth's normal take-charge approach.[8]

Elizabeth speaks again when Mary arrives at her house (v. 42). Her words are the first recognition of the special child that Mary carries in her womb, and the first of several blessings spoken throughout Luke's Infancy Narrative.[9]

But in Mary's case her words on two occasions are recorded. First, she gives an accepting response to the angel at the end of the angel's

8.   Reid, *Better Part*, p. 63.
9.   Reid, *Better Part*, p. 71.

visit (v. 38). Then she speaks to Elizabeth at Elizabeth's home, in her hymn of praise to God in vv. 46-55.

Then the second movement begins for each of the stories. The births are recorded, indicating the fulfillment of the promises made by the angel to both families. In Elizabeth's case the announcement is quite short: the child is born and the neighbors share the family's joy. Then the circumcision receives lengthy discussion, because that is the occasion when Zechariah regains his speech. Interestingly, his mother already knows that he will be named John, the name given him by the angel during his visit to Zechariah (vv. 57-80).

In Mary's case, this part has two divisions, like much of the first movement. The first part records Jesus' birth and the circumstances surrounding it, including the note about the census, to situate the birth at Bethlehem. The public witnesses to Jesus' birth are angels and shepherds, and the narrative describes their visits in much greater detail than it does in John's case. The circumcision and naming is given only a brief mention, including the reminder that the angel originally named the child (2.1-21). And the second division of this part describes the presentation in the Temple. The event is described, along with the sacrifice offered and the witness of two frequenters of the Temple. This clearly emphasizes the connection between Jesus and the Temple (2.22-40).

The second part in each case, the words spoken on the child's behalf, are all embedded in the birth and naming narratives. For John it is his father Zechariah who speaks in what the text identifies as a prophecy.[10] For Jesus it is first Simeon who praised God that Jesus has been born. He then speaks to Mary, predicting great things for her infant son. Finally the text records that Anna speaks. Without recording her words it recounts that she praises God and begins to speak about the child. Her presence in the story and her name, the Greek version of Hannah, bring clearly to mind the Samuel story. Like Hannah, she speaks in the public shrine, but unlike Hannah's, Anna's words are not recorded.

Finally, the two stories conclude with a brief mention of the boys' early years and first public appearances (1.80; 2.39-40, 41-52).

The parallel structure of the two stories illustrates the interweaving of their lives from their earliest childhoods.

---

10. Besides Zechariah, only John (1.76) and Anna (2.36) are identified as prophets until Jesus is so named in 9.28-36.

The Barren Mother Models in the Lukan Narrative

As in the Hannah stories, the plot of Luke's Infancy Narrative follows the type of the barren mother in the case of Elizabeth and Mary. Both women bore sons through divine intervention, then fulfilled the prescribed rituals to initiate their sons into their respective communities. Both sons served the people by carrying forward the Lord's promises to Israel. And both sons helped bring about significant transitions, John as herald and Jesus as founder of the kingdom of God.

Competition Model
In terms of the three models of the barren mother type, the Lukan narrative reconfigures the competition model to juxtapose two women who supported rather than competed with each other. But the model provides a useful way to look at the stories because their basic elements closely follow the model. The Lukan narrative involves two women who were relatives, but their stories remain separate at first. Then at the end of Gabriel's visit to Mary, he explained that her kinswoman Elizabeth had conceived, setting the stage for the two stories and the two women to come together.

Both women were childless, Elizabeth because she was barren and Mary because she was not yet married. The story involves two different husbands, Zechariah, who had been married to Elizabeth for many years, and Joseph, who was not yet wedded to Mary. Neither woman enjoyed a favored position over the other, nor did either man have two wives.

Through divine intervention Elizabeth conceived first and rejoiced at her condition, saying, 'This is what the Lord has done for me when he looked favorably on me and took away the disgrace I have endured among the people' (Lk. 1.25). Her joy alludes to that of Sarah, who exclaimed when Isaac was born, 'God has brought laughter for me; everyone who hears will laugh with me' (Gen. 21.6) and Rachel, who announced, 'God has taken away my reproach' (Gen. 30.23) when Joseph was born.

After the angel's visit to Zechariah he went next to Mary and told her that she would bear a son through divine intervention. After she heard the announcement of her own pregnancy she went to visit Elizabeth. Their meeting was one of mutual support, rather than conflict. Elizabeth rejoiced in her good fortune that her guest was mother of her Lord. The setting and words allude to the frequent occasions in the Hebrew Bible when the younger takes precedence over the older.[11]

Mary stayed with her relative three months. The details of those three months are left to the reader's imagination. But we can readily imagine the support the two women offered each other during their mutual period of waiting. Elisabeth Schüssler Fiorenza comments regarding the complex and problematic events, 'In Luke's account, the unwed pregnant Mary does not remain alone with her anxieties but seeks support from another pregnant woman, Elizabeth.'[12] Luke reports that when Elizabeth's son was born her neighbors and relatives rejoiced with her (Lk. 1.58). And when Mary's son was born the angel announced it to nearby shepherds, who went to visit him (2.8-20).

Promise Model

The narrative faithfully follows the promise model in the case of both Elizabeth and Mary. Elizabeth was barren (Lk. 1.7; see Gen. 11.30). Gabriel appeared to her husband Zechariah in the Temple while he was performing the offering of incense. The angel promised a son who would bring joy to them and to many. The child would be a nazirite and, filled with the Holy Spirit, would turn the people toward God, faithfulness and righteousness (1.13-17).[13]

In keeping with the promise model, Zechariah asked for some confirmation on account of the ages of his wife and himself (v. 18). In response the angel confirmed the announcement, declaring that Zechariah would remain mute until the events came to pass (vv. 19-20). (Zechariah's loss of speech can be understood on several levels, and will be discussed in detail below. Here in the promise model it functions as a sign of confirmation.)[14] The waiting crowd realized that Zechariah had 'seen a vision' when he emerged from the Temple unable to speak.

The promised son was born and was named 'John', which startled those in attendance because it was not a family name. The naming incident also provided the occasion for Zechariah to regain his speech, for

11. Brenner, *Israelite Woman*, p. 102.

12. E. Schüssler Fiorenza, J*esus: Miriam's Child, Sophia's Prophet* (New York: Continuum, 1994), p. 186.

13. While Luke's account does not mention Joseph, Matthew describes a dream in which the angel reassures Joseph about Mary's pregnancy in 1.18-25.

14. Brenner, *Israelite Woman*, pp. 103-104.

his mouth was opened after he agreed in writing, 'His name is John' (1.63). The events of John's birth incited fear among the neighbors, and caused them to wonder at the child's birth and about his future (vv. 65-66).

In Mary's case her unmarried but betrothed status was the reason for her childlessness. She was not barren, but the allusion to the type is clear. Gabriel appeared to her and announced that she would bear a son. He made several references to the child, linking him with the kingdom: he would be given David's throne, would reign over the house of Jacob, and his kingdom would have no end (vv. 26-33). Mary responded, not with the incredulity of those long married yet childless, but with the puzzlement of a virgin (v. 34). When the angel's reassurance attributed the events to divine activity, Mary acquiesced (vv. 35-38), the promised son was born, and he received the name 'Jesus' announced by Gabriel (2.7, 21).

Request Model

The request model fits the account of Zechariah and Elizabeth, but not that of Mary. When the angel visited Zechariah, his first words to the priest were, 'Do not be afraid, Zechariah, for your prayer has been heard. Your wife Elizabeth will bear you a son' (v. 13), thus acknowledging Zechariah's petition and offering the Lord's response.

But neither Mary nor Joseph requested a son at the time recorded in the story, which was before their marriage. Such requests were traditionally made after years of childless marriage.

People and Places in the Infancy Narrative

Various literary features support Luke's complex plot. The most evident of these is the greater number of characters. Not only are there two husbands, two wives and two babies; but also Gabriel, friends and relatives, as well as shepherds, teachers and all who were present at the various incidents in the Temple. The larger number of people provides a network of witnesses to the events recorded in the narrative, and the witness was often in the form of speech.

Speaking Witnesses

Many of the characters speak throughout the narrative. Their best-known speeches are the three hymns. Mary's song of praise resembles the Song of Hannah in several ways: its introduction refers explicitly to her personal receipt of divine favor, and names divine deeds on behalf of specific vulnerable groups (the lowly, the hungry and Israel).[15] The hymn specifies the rationale for the divine actions: to honor the promise to Israel's earliest ancestors and all their descendants, thereby including the Jewish community of her own day.

Zechariah also praises God in terms of the traditions and history of Israel: he refers to the divine promise to be the God of the people (1.68), David the king (v. 69), the prophets (v. 70), and the covenant with Abraham (vv. 72-73). In Zechariah's hymn the rationale for divine deeds is to enable the people to serve their God (vv. 74-75). Zechariah then speaks to his infant son, commissioning him as a prophet to prepare the way of the Most High (vv. 76-77). Zechariah then proclaims the dawning of a new era of light, life and peace made possible by divine mercy (vv. 78-79). Additional praise comes from Simeon in a statement resembling last words, in which he speaks of the infant Jesus as the personification of salvation for Israel and the world (2.29-32).

In addition, various people's words fill in the details of the plot and reflect on the meaning of the events. The words often allude to or quote the Hebrew Bible, linking the people and events in Luke's narrative with the history and traditions of Israel. Here I will discuss details of plot and meaning. Then I will consider links to the Hebrew Bible later in this chapter.

Elizabeth thanks God for removing from her the disgrace of barrenness. She welcomes Mary as her guest and 'mother of my Lord' (v. 43). Then at John's circumcision Elizabeth announces to the guests the name of their newborn child (1.60).

Mary responds to the angel's announcement of Jesus' birth with a question (v. 34). She sings the Magnificat in Elizabeth's presence, and questions Jesus in the Temple when he is 12 years old (2.48).[16] The text also records Mary's silence while she 'treasured all these words and

---

15. The term 'lowly' is a prominent motif in the Infancy Narrative. It will be discussed in detail below.

16. In light of the parallels in the stories of Hannah and of Mary and Elizabeth, it seems surprising that Mary, rather than Elizabeth, sang the Song. The issue preoccupied Lukan scholars in the first half of the twentieth century. See, for example, F. Spitta, 'Das Magnificat: Ein Psalm der Maria und nicht der Elisabeth', in *Theologische Abhandlung für H.J. Holtzmann* (Tübingen: J.C.B. Mohr, 1902).

pondered them in her heart' (2.19). The narrative comment seems to foreshadow events to come.[17]

Gabriel announces to Zechariah and Mary that they will have sons. The announcements identify him as a messenger in the spirit of the three men who visited Abraham. And they link together the two children as well as the two mothers.[18] The angel who announces the birth of Jesus to the shepherds is not identified in the text.

On two occasions the people at the Temple witness significant events. Those who observe Zechariah's loss of speech wonder at the meaning of his muteness. At the time of Jesus' presentation Simeon offers praise, blesses the family, then foretells that the child will serve as a catalyst during a period of division and realignment, and predicted suffering for Mary.

Anna's words on that occasion are not recorded, but the text recounts that she praises God and speaks about the child to 'all who were looking for the redemption of Israel' (2.36-38).

The first words the text ascribes to Jesus are spoken in the Temple when at the age of 12 he associates himself with 'his Father's House' in response to his mother's question (vv. 48-49). His ambiguous response suggests family ties beyond those into which he is born, and aspirations beyond his father's carpentry work.

John does not speak in the Infancy Narrative, but ch. 3 begins with his preaching about baptism. And Joseph remains silent and nearly invisible in Luke's narrative, except for a brief genealogical note (1.27), a comment about his journey to Bethlehem for the census, and a word about the amazement he shares with Mary at Simeon's words (2.33). In contrast, Matthew's account records that Joseph has a dream of a son to be born. The dream alleviates his anxiety about marrying Mary. An angel warns him to flee to Egypt, and an angel instructs him to return to Israel (Mt. 1.20-21; 2.13, 19-20).

The stories frequently use contrasts between characters. Just as Samuel's righteousness is contrasted with the corruption of the house of Eli (1 Sam. 2.11–4.22), several pairs of characters in the Lukan narrative serve as foils for each other. Zechariah and Mary are contrasted in that Zechariah can not speak with his wife Elizabeth during her

17. D. Daube, *The New Testament and Rabbinic Judaism* (New York: Arno, 1973), p. 319.

18. S.H. Ringe, *Luke* (Louisville, KY: Westminster/John Knox Press, 1995), p. 30.

pregnancy, but Mary journeys to visit her and speak with her about the meaning of both their pregnancies.[19] Elizabeth contrasts with Mary in terms of age. And just as the Hebrew Bible frequently reverses the roles of older and younger children, Luke portrays the younger Mary as superior to her older relative Elizabeth. John the Baptist and Jesus are contrasted insofar as John the prophet prepares the way for Jesus the Savior (Lk. 3.4-17). The contrasts characterize the different people as foils for each other. They also strengthen the theme of divine guidance at play in the lives of the people. In fact, the contrasts cut across the Testaments as well: Anna contrasts with Hannah in her lack of recorded speech.

Places in the Narrative

The number of locations where the events of the Lukan plot take place is also larger than in the Samuel narrative. The Infancy Narrative begins and ends at the Temple, focusing the various incidents around the center of the Jewish religion in Jesus' time.[20] In addition to the announcement that John would be born and the incident among the teachers when Jesus was 12 years old, the purification of Mary and the presentation of Jesus also occurred at the Temple.

Mary's home in Nazareth was the scene of the Annunciation, and the town remained the family home during Jesus's childhood. Elizabeth and John's home was in the hill country of Ain Karim. Mary traveled there to visit Elizabeth, and John's circumcision took place there. Joseph and Mary registered in Bethlehem, where they remained for the birth of Jesus. The action follows the pattern of 1 Samuel, in which the events alternated between the Shiloh shrine and the family home. Here the plot moves between the Temple and the homes of the two women. But among the three women, Elizabeth, Mary and Hannah, Mary was the only one whose home was the setting for the birth announcement.

Mary's Song

The words of praise Mary sang in Elizabeth's presence allude to the Song of Hannah in several ways. I will now discuss the Magnificat in detail, to illustrate the similarities between the two poems.

19. Ringe, *Luke*, p.31.
20. Johnson, *Luke*, pp. 14-15.

Genre, Structure and Content

After Elizabeth's greeting to Mary the narrative pauses and invites the reader to savor the meaning of the events and announcements through Mary's poetic hymn. The words sing in celebration of the God who gave a child to Mary and through him granted salvation to Israel. Various rhetorical and grammatical features contribute to the artistry of the whole. The first of these is its genre, which provides the framework of the poem and our consideration of it.

The poem's genre has been identified in various ways. For example, Hermann Gunkel classified it as an eschatological hymn, while Douglas Jones sees it as a mixed genre in keeping with the postexilic disintegration of psalm types. Heinz Schürmann calls the mix a combination of eschatological hymn and individual thanksgiving, noting that the mix may actually be an identifiable type. James Forestell classifies it as a hymn of thanksgiving for national salvation, spoken in the name of the daughter of Sion.[21] The variety of suggested genres speaks to the complexity and depth of the poem itself, which I call a hymn in keeping with the basic definition of that genre: it begins with introductory praise, then gives the reasons for praise.

The song follows.[22]

1.46	And Mary said, 'My soul magnifies the Lord,
47	and my spirit rejoices in God my Savior,
48	for he has looked with favor on the lowliness of his servant. Surely, from now on all generations will call me blessed;
49	for the Mighty One has done great things for me, and holy is his name.
50	His mercy is for those who fear him from generation to generation.
51	He has shown strength with his arm; he has scattered the proud in the thoughts of their hearts.
52	He has brought down the powerful from their thrones, and lifted up the lowly;

21. See J.T. Forestell, 'Old Testament Background of the Magnificat', *Marian Studies* 12 (1961), pp. 205-44 (225); H. Gunkel, 'Die Lieder in der Kindheitsgeschichte Jesu bei Lukas', in *Festgabe A. Von Harnack zum 70. Geburtstag dargebracht* (Tübingen: J.C.B. Mohr, 1921), pp. 43-60; D. Jones, 'The Background and Character of the Lukan Psalms', *JTS* 19 (1968), pp. 44-45; and H. Schürmann, *Das Lukasevangelium* (Herdeus theologischer Kommentar zum Neven Testament, 3.1; Freiburg: Herder, 1969), p. 71.

22. NRSV translation.

53   he has filled the hungry with good things, and sent the rich away
        empty.
54   He has helped his servant Israel, in remembrance of his mercy,
55   according to the promise he made to our ancestors, to Abraham and
        to his descendants forever.'

Analysis of the Song

The theme of praise permeates the poem's two stanzas, vv. 46-50 and
vv. 51-55. The first of these considers the meaning of God's gift for
Mary and the second broadens the thought to include the people of
Israel.[23]

The pattern of verbs in the hymn focuses on action and helps create
the two-stanza format.[24] Ten of the seventeen stichs begin with active
verbs. The two parallel introductory stichs in v. 47[25] both begin with

23. This division according to content and form follows R.C. Tannehill, 'The
Magnificat as Poem', *JBL* 93 (1974), pp. 263-75 (268).

24. Johnson notes Luke's use of speeches, typical of Hellenistic historians. He
delineates four stages of Mary's Song/speech: the reversal of Mary's condition
from lowliness to exaltation (vv. 46-49); a general statement of divine mercy to
those who fear him (v. 50); a recital of past and present reversals (vv. 51-53); and a
statement of how that mercy is now being shown to Israel in fulfillment of the
divine promise to Abraham (vv. 54-55) (*Luke*, p. 43). Ringe divides the Song into
two parts: the first addresses the immediate circumstances (vv. 46-49) and the
second celebrates divine deeds and ways in more general terms (vv. 50-55). The
second half contains three parts: the first (v. 50) and last (vv. 54-55) celebrate
divine mercy. The end specifically celebrates God's faithfulness to divine promises
and to those to whom God is joined in covenant, a central theme for Luke. The
second of the three parts details the results of the divine show of strength (vv. 51-
53). Two sets of contrasting parallels or reversals develop the theme. The first
juxtaposes the 'proud' and 'powerful' with the 'lowly'. The second contrasts the
hungry and the rich. The categories express the coming together of economic and
political opposites. The two outer sections temper the center one by placing God's
reversals in the context of divine mercy. And the center section prevents an overly
sentimental understanding of God's mercy: this is a God who turns the status quo
upside down. The Magnificat's similarity to the Song of Hannah affirms the
continuity Luke sees in God's commitment to the people. See Ringe, *Luke*, pp. 35-
36. Samuel Terrien delineates a structure of four strophes surrounding the core
v. 51. He entitles the strophes 'The First Daughter of the Church' (vv. 46-48); 'The
Compassion of God' (vv. 49-50); 'The Mother of Revolution' (vv. 52-53); and
'The Sacrality of the Future' (vv. 54-55). See his *The Magnificat: Musicians as
Biblical Interpreters* (New York: Paulist Press, 1995), pp. v-vii, xx.

25. This verse numbering follows the NRSV, in which the introductory 'And

verbs, as do vv. 48a, 49a, 51a and b, 52 a and b, 54a, and 55a. (Conjunctions are not counted in this schema.) These initial verbs set the tone of action and triumphal strength that fills the poem. In the remaining stichs, vv. 49b-50 and 55b are non-verbal. The verb in v. 48b appears later in the stich and is the only verb in the future tense in the poem, v. 53a and 53b begin with participles followed by verbs, and v. 54b begins with a participle followed by a noun. This verbal structure highlights the division into two stanzas: the break in the pattern of initial verbs at vv. 49b-50 offers a pause in the action and an opportunity to reflect on it, just as the entire poem offers a meditative pause in the action of the Infancy Narrative. And the pause prepares the reader for the shift in focus that begins in v. 51.

The verbs form patterns of formal parallelism that support the meaning. The poem begins with two synonymous stichs that announce the theme of the song and personalize it as to speaker and object. The repetition of sounds in the first two syllables of the verbs adds a rhythmic cadence to the introductory words of praise. Verses 48a and 49a both begin with 'for', highlighting the reasons for Mary's praise and calling attention to the contrast between the lowly servant of v. 48 and the Mighty One's great things in v. 49. The two 'for' clauses set in relief v. 48b, which broadens the significance of the divine act from a personal gift for Mary to an event that will reverberate throughout the future among all people. The word 'lowliness' appears in v. 48 and 'lowly' occurs in v. 52, linking the themes of the two stanzas. In the earlier verse it describes the 'servant' (v. 48) who is contrasted with the 'Lord' in v. 47. In the second instance 'lowly' contrasts with 'powerful' in the same verse. And 'powerful' (δυνάστας) is related to 'Mighty One' (δυνατός) in v. 49. Again the pairs link the two stanzas, and also contrast God the savior with the powerful oppressors of Israel.

The non-verbal vv. 49b and 50 break the pattern of stichs that begin with verbs, creating a pause in the action and inviting reflection on the meaning of what has just been said. The motif of the generations introduced in v. 48b recurs and is repeated in v. 50b, expanding the recipients of divine mercy beyond Mary to all who fear the Lord. Divine mercy is mentioned in vv. 50 and 54, in the conclusions to both stanzas. Its first use refers to Mary and the second to Israel, expanding the scope of divine mercy from the individual who praises God in the first stanza

Mary said' is v. 46 and the synonymous two-stich words of initial praise are v. 47. The remainder of the poem is numbered the same as the Greek.

to Israel the divine servant, the focus of the second stanza.

Verse 51 shifts abruptly from celebration of divine mercy to affirmation of God's power while repetitions link the two stanzas. Verses 51 and 52 begin in synonymous parallel, without conjunctions or articles. This creates a staccato effect heightened by the guttural and hard sounds, highlighting the divine ability to accomplish these mighty deeds. The words 'strength' in v. 51 and 'powerful' in v. 52a heighten the image of divine power conveyed by the verses. And the anthropomorphic divine 'arm' strengthens the graphic presentation of divine strength.[26] The verb 'did' in v. 51a links the stich with v. 49a. The two verbs are followed by different objects, both connoting great and powerful deeds.

Verses 51b and 52a name in synonymous form the divine mighty deeds that bring down the arrogant and mighty. The list resumes in v. 53a, which shows God's power over the wealthy. While vv. 51b, 52a and 53b refer to the divine deeds against those who oppress the people, vv. 52b, 53a and 54a antithetically name God's acts on behalf of the lowly, the hungry and servant Israel. The six stichs thus form a thought pattern 'aabbab', linking the contrasts and highlighting the extent of divine power, which reverses extremes at both ends of the social spectrum.

The initial position of the participles in v. 53ab underlines the two socioeconomic extremes over which God has power: the hungry and the rich. By relating the two words in that way, the song broadens the meaning of 'hungry' beyond the literal, to include those who long for many forms of fuller life.

Then, just as the poem pauses after the recital of actions in the first stanza, it takes a breath at v. 54b, reflecting on the significance of the divine deeds and relating them to the first stanza by repeating 'mercy'. The initial participle in v. 54b elaborates on the thought of v. 54a and calls on two major themes in Israel's tradition, 'remembering' and 'mercy', in celebrating the Lord's help to Israel. Verse 55 then continues the reflection on Israel's traditions. Its initial verb is followed by an indirect object, then two additional indirect objects in apposition with the first. The cluster of nouns invites reflection on the number of ancestors throughout Israel's history. It also recapitulates the theme of 'generations' from the first stanza, referring explicitly to God's

26. The word 'arm' recalls the anthropomorphisms in describing divine deeds during the Exodus (Exod. 15.12; Deut. 26.8; Ps. 136.12).

gratuitous promise to Abraham and his descendants. God's gift of a child to Mary is thus added to the long list of divine interventions throughout Israel's history in fulfillment of the original promise.[27]

The verse also brings the Song full circle: it begins with focus on Mary the individual, broadens to include all Israel, and ends with Abraham the individual. Thus Mary, the most recent recipient of a divine gift of a son, is linked with Abraham, the first recipient of God's promise of offspring. The association is strengthened by Gabriel's words to Mary, 'Nothing will be impossible with God', which recalls the Lord's words to Abraham, 'Is anything too wonderful for the Lord?' (Gen. 18.14). Just as the narrative links Mary with Sarah the barren mother, the Song links Mary with Sarah's husband Abraham, making her a new symbol of the people Israel. (See also Gen. 12.3; 15.2, 6; 16.11; 18.3).[28]

Zechariah's and Simeon's Words

A detailed consideration of Zechariah's and Simeon's poems is beyond the scope of this study. But I will briefly outline them, to note how carefully they are woven into their context. S.H. Ringe divides Zechariah's hymn into two parts: the first (vv. 68-75) praises God who has 'looked favorably' on the people. Its use of both past and future tenses encompasses all of time in God's care. The second (vv. 76-79) speaks to John's task of preparing the people to receive 'the one who is to come'.[29]

Simeon's words allude to the testamentary form insofar as he declares his vision for how life will continue after his death. For Simeon, Jesus' coming represents a future of salvation for Israel and all people.[30]

Luke's Use of the Hebrew Bible in the Infancy Narrative

The final verse of the hymn explicitly relates Mary to the history and traditions of Israel. Other allusions and references to the Hebrew Bible

27. Forestell, *Background*, p. 238.

28. R. Laurentin, *Structure et théologie de Luc I–II* (Paris: Librairie Lecoffre, 1957), p. 85.

29. Ringe, *Luke*, pp. 38-39. See the detailed discussion of the poem in S. Farris, *The Hymns of Luke's Infancy Narratives* (Sheffield: JSOT Press, 1985), pp. 127-42.

30. See Farris, *Hymns*, pp. 143-50 for a careful analysis of the speech.

permeate the language and thought of the prayer and the entire Infancy Narrative. The themes and values they connote relate the events in the narrative to the whole sweep of Israel's history from the time of Abraham to the Roman Empire.

The Magnificat's Use of the Hebrew Bible
I will consider the use of the Hebrew Bible first in the Magnificat, then throughout the narrative. In the Song the references uncover layers of evocative meaning in the poetry, the first of which is the hymn's similarity to the LXX version of the Song of Hannah. Both hymns, in keeping with their genre, follow the basic form of praise to God, followed by the reasons for praise. And both hymns use antithetic parallelism to celebrate the Lord's reversal of the fortunes of the mighty and the weak (1 Sam. 2.4; Lk. 1.52), the hungry and the satisfied (1 Sam. 2.4; Lk. 1.53), the rich and the poor (1 Sam. 2.7-8, Lk. 1.53). Specific words and themes are similar; for example both refer to God as holy (1 Sam. 2.2; Lk. 1.49) and both condemn arrogance (1 Sam. 1.3; Lk. 1.51).[31]

Several verses of the Magnificat either quote or allude to biblical passages. A cluster of references reveals two prominent motifs: the 'lowly' and 'divine mercy.' For example, v. 47 resembles Hab. 3.18: 'Yet I will rejoice in the Lord; I will exult in the God of my salvation.' Verse 48a recalls Deut. 26.7: 'The Lord heard our voice and saw our affliction' (עֲנְיֵנוּ). The motif of God's regard for the lowly also appears in 2 Esd. 9.45: 'God heard your servant, and looked upon my low estate.' Lk. 1.49 recalls Deut. 10.21: 'He is your God, who has done for you [Israel] these great and awesome things', contrasting divine deeds with the status of the people. And Lk. 1.52-53 is similar to Dan. 4.37, which reports that Nebuchadnezzar praises God who 'is able to bring low those who walk in pride'.

These references highlight the status of the Christians under Roman rule in the time of Luke. The term 'lowly' (עֲנָוִים, ταπεινούς) connotes 'humiliated' or 'marginalized', the result of personal or communal affliction or of one's failure to live according to the code of honor of the society. In the case of women it could describe one who was childless or who had been raped. Under the Roman Empire the term took on the spiritual connotation of a person or group who had no place in the

---

31. The Song resembles Miriam's words in Exod. 15 as well. See Reid, *Better Part*, p. 102.

dominant group, and 'belonged' only to God. This identity was based on fidelity to the covenant. The עניים trusted that God would reward their fidelity by removing their oppressed status. Mary's use of the word announces her solidarity with these 'lowly' ones who longed to be included with the recipients of God's promises to the people.[32] In fact the motif permeates the entire Infancy Narrative.

Mary celebrates divine mercy (ἔλεος, חסד) on 'those who fear [God] from generation to generation' (Lk. 1.50) and on Israel in v. 54. In fact, the Greek term is used in the LXX to translate two Hebrew terms, חסד (steadfast love) and רחם (mercy). The similarity between Mary's words and the speeches of Moses in Deuteronomy indicates that חסד is the preferred word here. Moses' speeches actually bring together three motifs: divine חסד upon many generations as a reward for human faithfulness. He asserts, 'I am a jealous God...showing steadfast love to the thousandth generation of those who love me and keep my commandments' (Deut. 5.9-10); 'It was because the Lord loved you and kept the oath that he swore to your ancestors, that the Lord has brought you out with a mighty hand, and redeemed you from the house of slavery, from the hand of Pharaoh king of Egypt. Know therefore that the Lord your God is God, the faithful God who maintains covenant loyalty (חסד) with those who love him and keep his commandments, to a thousand generations' (7.8-9); and 'If you heed these ordinances, by diligently observing them, the Lord your God will maintain with you the covenant loyalty (חסד) that he swore to your ancestors' (7.12).

Mary also relates God's mercy to divine memory in Lk. 1.54. The Hebrew Bible is replete with God's promises to remember the people (Gen. 9.15-16; Lev. 26.42, 45; Isa. 43.18, 25); with the people's pleas that God remember the promises to their ancestors (Jer. 14.21); or remember the people (Lam. 5.1). In Psalm 136 the people celebrate their own memory of divine guidance throughout the 40 years in the wilderness.

The promises are linked to the people's faithfulness (Deut. 6.3; 26.18-19; 29.10-15; Josh. 23.14-16; Ps. 119.41-48; Isa. 63.11; Hos. 7.2; Amos 1.9). The people plead with God not only to reward their faithfulness but also to punish the arrogant. For example in Jdt. 6.19 the people pray, 'O Lord God of heaven, see [the Assyrians'] arrogance, and have pity on our people in their humiliation, and look kindly today on the faces of those who are consecrated to you.'

32. See Forestell, *Background*, pp. 211-12, and Ringe, *Luke*, p. 34.

On another level, the epithets of God in the Song appear in the narrative as attributes of Mary's child. Mary called God 'holy' in 1.49; the angel announces to her that her son will be holy in 1.35. Mary addresses the Deity as 'Lord' in 1.47; Elizabeth speaks to Mary as 'mother of my Lord' in 1.43. Mary refers to God as 'Savior' in 1.47; the angel announces to the shepherds that a savior is born (2.11). This repetition of divine epithets joins the narrative and song into a unified whole, expressing Luke's belief in the unity between God and the child.

And the revolutionary deeds of God recited in the Magnificat are also named in the Beatitudes (6.20-26).[33] This similarity links God with the people who imitate divine acts in their lives.

Use of the Hebrew Bible in the Narrative

Luke's reliance on the Bible is not limited to the Magnificat. The entire Infancy Narrative is replete with allusions and direct references to the Hebrew Scriptures.[34] The prevalence of women recalls the story of Moses' birth in Exod. 1.1–2.10. And Elizabeth and Zechariah are described as righteous (δίκαιοι, Lk. 1.6), as is Job (1.1, LXX). Elizabeth expresses her gratitude that the shame of barrenness has been removed from her in words that recall Sarah's laughter under similar circumstances (Lk. 1.25; Gen. 18.15).

Gabriel's words to Mary in Lk. 1.32-33 carry forward the promise to David in 2 Sam. 7.12-16.[35] And the annunciation alludes to three prophetic texts: Zeph. 3.14-17; Joel 2.21-27; Zech. 9.9-10. All three are addressed to daughter Zion, the personification of Israel; all of them contain the command to rejoice and not to fear; and two of the three announce that the Lord is coming to reside in Zion (this is not found in Zech. 9, but does appear in Zech. 2.14). Both Zephaniah and Zechariah then refer to the Lord's coming as king and savior.[36] In fact, Zeph. 3.15, 17 describe the Lord's presence among the people 'in the womb' (בקרב). (See also Exod. 33.3, 5 for the same verb use).[37]

Also in terms of plot elements, the visits by Gabriel follow the

---

33, Johnson, *Luke*, p. 44.

34. Laurentin's treatment of the references and their meaning is particularly helpful. For his discussion of the use of the Hebrew Bible in the Magnificat, see Laurentin, *Structure*, pp. 82-86.

35. Laurentin, *Structure*, pp. 71-73.

36. Laurentin, *Structure*, pp. 64-67.

37. Laurentin, *Structure*, p. 70.

pattern of calls in Israel's traditions: as with Abraham (Gen. 17.15-22), Moses (Exod. 3.1–4.17) and Jeremiah (Jer. 1.4-10), an announcement is made in a significant location, the recipient raises an objection which the messenger overrides, and the recipient finally accepts the call. For Zechariah, acceptance seems not to come until the naming of his son at the time of circumcision, when he regains the use of his voice (Lk. 1.63).

Mary's acquiescence to Gabriel's announcement resembles the formulas by which Abraham and Isaiah accept their commissions from God (Lk. 1.38; Gen. 22.1; Isa. 6.8). Zechariah's commission to his son John recalls Isa. 40.3. And when John begins to preach he speaks in the same vein.

Uzziah's words in Jdt. 13.18, 'O daughter, you are blessed by the Most High God above all other women on earth', are reflected in Elizabeth's greeting to Mary in Lk. 1.42. The language of Elizabeth's exclamation of recognition resembles David's celebration at the entry of the Ark into Jerusalem (2 Sam. 6.9). And the three-month stays of the Ark and of Mary (2 Sam. 6.11; Lk. 1.56) are recounted in similar language. Laurentin observes the allusion to the Ark's journey up to Jerusalem: Mary visits Elizabeth as a stage on her journey to Jerusalem with the child Jesus within her.[38]

Luke's description of the journey to Bethlehem parallels Micah's words about that city in 5.1-5. And the manger where they lay Jesus alludes to the basket in which the infant Moses is hidden (Exod. 2.3).[39]

And Simeon's reference to Jesus as 'a light for revelation to the Gentiles' (2.32) recalls Isa. 42.6, 'I have given you as a covenant to the people, a light to the nations.' Simeon's prediction of Jesus' future and Mary's suffering resembles the Lord's words to Rebekah, 'two peoples born of you shall be divided' in Gen. 25.23, and the Lord's commission to Jeremiah, 'See, today I appoint you over nations and over kingdoms, to pluck up and to pull down, to destroy and to overthrow, to build and to plant' (Jer. 1.10).[40] It also brings to mind Isaiah's words about God, 'He will become a sanctuary, a stone one strikes against; for both houses of Israel he will become a rock one stumbles over—a trap and a snare for the inhabitants of Jerusalem. And many among them shall

38. Laurentin, *Structure*, pp. 89-90.
39. Brenner, *Israelite Woman*, p. 104.
40. Ringe, *Luke*, p. 46.

tumble; they shall fall and be broken; they shall be snared and taken' (Isa. 8.14-15).[41]

Mary 'treasured all these words and pondered them in her heart' (Lk. 2.19), recalling that Jacob 'kept the matter (of Joseph's dreams) in mind' (Gen. 37.11). And Elizabeth dropped out of the narrative by the end of the Infancy Narrative, as did Hannah in 1 Samuel.

These references link the story of Jesus' birth with those of Israel's earlier leaders, and highlight the historical continuity and divine guidance the people had enjoyed since the time of Abraham. And just as Abraham was the original symbol of the people of promise, Mary was that symbol for Luke.[42] In this way Luke introduced a new kind of divine inbreaking among the people, by which the 'barren mother' evolved into the mother of God who lived among the people in human form.[43] Mary continued the tradition of overturning the prevailing categories in the logic of the reign of God by housing the Deity in her womb. Jesus' birth and childhood were relatively obscure in keeping with that logic, and the Magnificat celebrates God's love for the humble and the poor.[44]

The narrative uses several allusions and levels of meaning in describing Zechariah's muteness. On one level, it is the sign of divine confirmation found in call narratives. On another level it is the punishment Zechariah receives for not believing the angel's announcement. And thirdly it links Zechariah with Ezekiel, whom God commanded to eat the divine word, then rendered mute because of the rebelliousness of the house of Israel (Ezek. 3.26). In Ezekiel's case his muteness is thought to represent the unalterability and inevitability of the word of God; and the prophet's actions, influenced by the words he had consumed, became his message. Ezekiel remained mute until the precondition was met: the city fell (33.22).[45] His muteness also reversed his usual role of speaker and teacher, just as Elizabeth's pregnancy reversed her childlessness. Zechariah regained his speech when

41. Laurentin, *Structure*, pp. 89-90.

42. Laurentin, *Structure*, p. 85.

43. Callaway, *Sing*, pp. 100-101. See also Brown, *Birth*, pp. 304, 521-24.

44. Laurentin, *Structure*, p. 83; Ringe, *Luke*, p. 12.

45. E.F. Davis, 'Swallowing Hard: Reflections on Ezekiel's Dumbness', in J.C. Exum (ed.), *Signs and Wonders: Biblical Texts in Literary Focus* (Semeia Studies; Atlanta: Scholars Press, 1989), pp. 217-37.

he consented to the name of the child, just as Mary's consent empower-ed her to speak. His punishment and later inspiration serve in the narrative to illuminate notions of obedience and total faith in Providence.

Luke's use of references and allusions to the Hebrew Bible conveys an idea closely linked to it, but radically different: Luke recounts the birth story of Jesus who is God like YHWH.[46]

Luke's Use of the Hannah Narrative
The foregoing analysis of the Infancy Narrative and Magnificat high-lights the dependence of the Lukan text on the Hebrew Bible in terms of values, motifs and vocabulary. It converges to a high degree with the Hannah narrative in 1 Samuel.

In both 1 Samuel and Luke the speakers and their words are situated within history. Hannah gave birth to Samuel during the period of the judges, and he instituted the Israelite monarchy. And the Lukan births are noted in relation to the Roman Empire. It is puzzling, however, that there is no record of a Roman census in Palestine for the years sur-rounding Jesus' birth, suggesting that, while Luke reported time in relation to current events, those events served a purpose other than his-torical. The purpose of a census was to bring the tax rolls up to date, and in that frame of reference the link between the census and the circumstances of Jesus' birth seems to identify his coming with tighten-ing of repression of subject peoples by the Roman Empire.[47] And the time of Gabriel's visit to Mary is given in relation to Elizabeth's preg-nancy: in the sixth month (1.26). In Samuel's case, the time can be adduced in relation to the capture of the Ark by the Philistines at Ebenezer and Aphek, and its subsequent journeys until it was housed in Kiriath-jearim for 20 years. Both accounts are careful to describe events in the context of the world of their time, anchoring them firmly within the life of the people and relating them to the political and socio-economic circumstances within which they took place.

All three stories involve promises: Hannah made a vow that her son would be dedicated to divine service (1 Sam. 1.11), the angel promised Zechariah that the nazirite son to be born to him and Elizabeth would turn the people toward righteousness (Lk. 1.15-16), and Mary was assured that her son would inherit the throne of David (v. 32). As the

46. Laurentin, *Structure*, p. 92.
47. Ringe, *Luke*, pp. 40-41.

discussion of the promise model shows, Hannah's vow to God is unique among the many instances of visits by divine messengers to husband or wife. And the promises to Mary are the most problematic: it is one thing to have a child in one's old age by divine intervention, but quite another when the woman is still unmarried.[48] Artist Lorenzo Lotto captured the complexity of the moment in his portrayal of the fear, not only of Mary but also of the fleeing cat in his painting *Annunciation*.[49]

Each promise clearly specified that the child would serve the people in a significant public way. The service each would perform reflects the ancient Near Eastern ideal of concern for the more vulnerable members of society, articulated in early law codes as the particular responsibility of the king, and in Israel's law as a mandate for the entire community (Exod. 2.21-23) under divine guidance.[50] David summarized his reign in terms of divine protection, proclaiming to God, 'You deliver a humble people' (2 Sam. 22.28) after all his battles with Israel's enemies. Isaiah's promises for the new king carry the same theme: 'He will establish and uphold [the throne of David] with justice and with righteousness' (Isa. 9.7) and 'with righteousness he shall judge the poor, and decide with equity for the meek of the earth' (11.4). The three sons, particularly Samuel and Jesus, would usher in new eras of justice. Their mothers' hymns voiced that hope and celebrated that promise.

The stories attribute the births of the sons to divine intervention on behalf of the women: Hannah was barren but relatively young because after Samuel she gave birth to three more sons and two daughters (1 Sam. 2.21); Elizabeth was barren and elderly, and Mary was not yet married. All three sons represent divine gifts to the women, but on a much larger scale the mothers and sons all represent special inbreakings of God in the life of all the people at significant moments in their history. Hannah and Samuel forged a new relationship between God and the people during the formation of the kingdom of Israel. And in Luke's vision, Elizabeth, John, Mary and Jesus forged another new

48. J. Schaberg, 'Luke', in C.A. Newsom and S.H. Ringe (eds.), *The Women's Bible Commentary* (Louisville: Westminster/John Knox Press, 1992), pp. 283-84.

49. L. Lotto, *Annunciation* (Recanati, Pinacoteca Civica, c. 1534).

50. For instance, the epilogue to the Code of Hammurabi states, 'In order that the strong might not oppress the weak, that justice might be dealt the orphan (and) the widow...I wrote my precious words on my stela...I set it up in order to administer the law of the land, to prescribe the ordinances of the land, to give justice to the oppressed...' (see *ANET*, epilogue, ll. 60-80, p. 178).

relationship between God and the people in the introduction of the kingdom of God. Both transitions represented a dramatic shift in the manner of God's presence among the people. And both offered the people hope that the future would correct the oppressive situations of those who remained faithful to God. And in the Hannah story, divine inbreaking takes place at her request rather than by gratuitous divine act. The lack of human initiative in Luke's narrative highlights the uniqueness of Hannah's initiative and its effect on the history of Israel, and underscores divine action in the Infancy Narrative.

The narratives report that all three sons grew not only chronologically but in spirit as well: Samuel grew 'in stature and in favor with the Lord and with the people' (2.26); John the Baptist 'grew and became strong in spirit' (Luke 1.80); and Jesus 'grew and became strong, filled with wisdom; and the favor of God was upon him' (2.40). With these words the reader is assured that the three were guided by the Deity whose commission they fulfilled.

Divine Inbreakings in the Stories

Both stories involve the inbreaking of something new in the life of the community: Samuel instituted the kingdom of Israel by negotiating with God and the people, and anointing Saul and David under divine guidance. Jesus instituted the kingdom of God through teaching and healing. Perhaps Luke linked his Infancy Narrative tightly with Israel's long history of divine presence and guidance, then departed from the literary conventions in order to express his belief in a new kind of divine coming among the people.

Both of these changes were closely related to the sociopolitical realities of the day, but also involved new kinds of presence of God among the people. For the Israelites on the verge of monarchy, the question from a religious point of view was how to assure themselves that the community and covenant would continue through the mediation of a human king. The community described by Luke faced the opposite question as they grappled with the challenges posed by the life and teachings of Jesus: he was described in royal terms and spoke of a kingdom in the ideal sense of the term, but was an outsider among the political powers of the day.

But not so with regard to cult. Both Jesus and John were explicitly associated with the cult by reason of the events of their lives that took place in the Temple. John's birth was announced to Zechariah while he was performing the incense offering there, Simeon and Anna spoke in praise and blessing when Jesus was presented in the Temple, and the first recorded words of Jesus were spoken in the Temple. The same had been true of Samuel: Hannah visited the Shiloh shrine to ask for a son, she took him there with Eli in fulfillment of her vow, and it was there that God called him to be a prophet (1 Sam. 3.20).

All three birth stories highlight the divine role in the birth of a child, and in doing so, allude to God as divine mother. The three mothers assisted in giving birth to new eras in Israel, acting in the image of the divine mother who gives birth to new forms of divine presence among the people. The stories also challenge traditional meanings of status and identity. For women, identity was reckoned in relation to father, husband or oldest son. And for a married woman status depended on having a son. But Elkanah challenged that understanding when he questioned Hannah, 'Am I not more to you than ten sons?' (1 Sam. 1.8) Luke also challenged the traditional definitions by his declaration, 'My mother and my brothers are those who hear the word of God and do it' (Lk. 8.21). In fact, Mary's willingness to accept her child supports the importance of obedience within the Lukan context.[51]

Wealth and Poverty in the Stories

Both 1 Samuel and Luke's Gospel address the meaning and value of wealth and poverty. In the Samuel account, Hannah's vulnerability was caused by her childlessness but not her socioeconomic situation. She belonged to a family of some means: she was one of Elkanah's two wives, a situation that implies that her husband could afford to provide for both of them. And when she went to Shiloh to fulfill her vow she took generous offerings from the family holdings: a three-year-old bull (the Greek text reads 'three bulls'), an ephah of flour, and a skin of wine (1 Sam. 1.24). Hannah's words in her Song proclaim an end to poverty by divine deed. True, by the end of Solomon's reign poverty remained an aspect of the division of labor and the socioeconomic inequities of his regime (1 Kgs 9.15-28). But it ultimately provoked the rebellion which destroyed the united monarchy. And the eighth-century prophets continued to decry those inequities and the oppression inherent in them (e.g. Isa. 1.16-17; Amos 2.6-8; Mic. 2.1-2).

---

51. Trible, *Rhetoric*, pp. 35-38.

In Luke's account, on the other hand, while Elizabeth and Zechariah probably lived comfortably, with the social status associated with priesthood, Joseph's only identification was that he belonged to the house of David.[52] His genealogical roots were the reason for the trip to Bethlehem. Their child was born in poverty; their offering at his presentation was that of the poor: 'a pair of turtledoves or two young pigeons' (Lk. 2.24). Mary's Magnificat praised the God who feeds the hungry and Zechariah's words spoke of redemption in the traditional sense.

But elsewhere in Luke's gospel poverty is presented as problematic. For example, the economically poor and socially marginalized shepherds proclaimed the good news of Jesus' birth. (Luke does not mention magi in his Infancy Narrative.[53]) Their role supports Luke's theme of Jesus, salvation of the עניים. But several words of Jesus seem to encourage poverty as an ideal. Some examples are the beatitude, 'Blessed are you who are poor, for yours is the kingdom of God' (Lk. 6.20; Cf. Mt. 5.3); the requisites for discipleship: homelessness, rejection of family, rejection of the past (Lk. 9.57-62); and the instructions to the 70 who preceded Jesus in his travels to the towns: they were to take no purse, bag or sandals (10.1-4). While in the Samuel account and Luke's Infancy Narrative elimination of poverty characterizes the kingdom of Israel, elsewhere Luke seems to idealize poverty as an inherent aspect of faith.

But on a more subtle level, for Luke the problem was not poverty as such, but the imbalance between the lives of the poor and vulnerable and those of the wealthy and influential. His Gospel comes from a time when the Church was moving from a reform movement on the fringe to an institution within the Roman Empire. It was not yet an institution 'of' power, as in the time of Constantine, but an institution 'related to' power that was looking toward its own long-term needs.

In that context, for Luke the divine agenda differed from the empire's political accommodation and economic conservatism. Luke set aside the prevailing mentality, and celebrated the marginalized people's initiatives to take control of their lives.[54] Among the marginalized, women

---

52. See also Mt. 1.1-16.
53. Ringe, *Luke*, p. 44; and see Mt. 2.
54. Ringe, *Luke*, pp. 9-10.

were an important subset for Luke. Their exaltation in the Infancy Narrative, and particularly in the Magnificat reflects the theology of the ענוים as the people of God, and the accompanying reversal of values that characterizes the kingdom of God.

Chapter 6

DESIRE AND DESIGN

The foregoing discussion of Hannah in the different versions and appropriations offers portraits that remain similar in many ways, but diverge significantly from the narrative in 1 Samuel. In this chapter I will consider the similarities and shifts with regard to each of the three interweaving themes named in the Introduction, and how they create the overall shifts in meaning. Then I will offer suggestions for resignifying the stories according to contemporary concerns.

The Barren Mother Type in the Stories

First, the literary theme of the barren mother type scene illustrates the sometimes subtle changes in Hannah's actions and characterization in the different versions. According to the competition model, the biblical story and *Biblical Antiquities* highlight Hannah's remaining above the fray, 1 Samuel by depicting her silence and *Biblical Antiquities* by emphasizing Peninnah's taunts. Luke's Infancy Narrative, on the other hand, calls attention to the cooperation and mutual support that Mary and Elizabeth shared.

The promise model underscores the biblical Hannah's divergence from the type insofar as she made, rather than received, the promise or had it made by someone else on her behalf. And it illustrates the complex and problematic bestowal of two promises in *Biblical Antiquities*, according to which at first everyone except Hannah was promised by God that she would bear a son who would be the next leader. Then she herself was promised by Eli that she would bear a son, only to learn at the time of his dedication that Samuel had been promised to all the people before she asked for him. The narrative specifies that God named the child Samuel. But Luke's Infancy Narrative adheres completely to the model, highlighting the divine role in the births of John and Jesus.

The request model likewise illustrates the biblical Hannah's initiative insofar as she made the request on her own behalf, and did so in a public time and place. In *Pseudo-Philo*'s work, the promises mentioned above were both the result of requests made to God, first by all the people for a leader, then by Hannah for a son. But Hannah's request is diminished from that of the biblical narrative. Here the reason for her request is to take away her unworthiness, and no vow accompanies her prayer. Luke's Infancy Narrative specifies that Zechariah, but not Mary or Joseph, prayed for a son. The lack of request on their part is understandable because they were not yet married at the time of the announcement of a son to Mary. But it also reinforces Luke's theme of divine initiative at work.

All these changes highlight the dignity of Hannah and her later counterparts. The women are portrayed as strong mothers who nurture their biological and spiritual offspring according to the traditions of Israel. Thus they enable divine inbreakings within the communities in which the stories were composed. In addition, within each model the specific shifts in plot focus attention on particular motifs within the different stories. Competition loses its power and becomes one-sided in the Hannah stories, then develops into cooperation in Luke's Infancy Narrative. Promises and requests are the means by which divine purpose are revealed.

Divine and Human Initiative

Within the barren mother type scene the theological theme of divine guidance and human initiative is expressed. The variations illustrate the different weights given to divine and human causality in the stories.

At one end of the divine–human continuum, Luke's Infancy Narrative attributes the birth of the son entirely to God. At the other extreme, the biblical Hannah initiates the request, makes it in a public place and time, reinforces her plea with a vow to return the son to the Lord, and fulfills her vow at the proper time. And *Pseudo-Philo*'s Hannah falls between the other two on the continuum: she makes her request for a son in more complicated circumstances and in a less confident way than her biblical counterpart, with no accompanying promises, after the child had already been promised to all the people.

But all four Songs focus on divine action. While their specific contents and sociopolitical contexts reflect the particular concerns of each group, all express the conviction that God provides for the needs of the people. The details of each Song and narrative illustrate the processes and products of early biblical interpretation.

Early Biblical Interpretation

The four stories illustrate the third theme, early biblical interpretation, in its processes and its products. Each of the later versions is based on assumptions and concerns relevant to its time and place of composition. These influence the plot and characterization as well as the particular themes woven into the different versions of the narrative and Song. And in each case the result attests to the ongoing efforts of biblical interpreters to provide meaning for a contemporary audience or readership.

The story in 1 Samuel highlights the efforts of Hannah to improve her own situation and that of all who visited the Shiloh shrine. And it attests to the eagerness of Israel's exiles to find assurance of divine guidance in the midst of their losses to the Babylonians, and in spite of the events that precipitated them.

Biblical Antiquities articulates the efforts of the people to grasp the idea of life after death and the related concept of reward and punishment for one's actions, during the time when the Roman government's oppression of the people offered little opportunity for rewards during this life.

The Song in the *Targum of the Prophets* reflects a similar effort on the part of the people to find reassurance that God was guiding them, and especially their leaders, throughout their history, in spite of Roman oppression.

Luke's Infancy Narrative expresses the conviction that Jesus and the movement he started were rooted solidly in the traditions of Israel. The allusions and references to Israel's history, literature and religious practices highlight the people's belief that the newly founded kingdom of heaven was integrally related to the kingdom of Israel.

Contemporary Resignification of the Stories

These interpretations invite present-day readers to retell the Hannah story in order to address contemporary situations of oppression and corruption as well as to influence and be influenced by the Deity and to change the course of history. The stories highlight the Western tradition of asking God for what one wants in the conviction that requests are heard and granted. That assurance relies on the certitude that the Deity continually guides the affairs of life.

Specific retellings might focus on significant elements of the early stories. For example, the biblical Hannah took bold steps to improve her situation, asking God for what she wanted, making and fulfilling a promise to accomplish a needed change. She remained focused on her goal, refusing to be distracted by the difficulties that arose. And Luke's Mary graciously received what she was given and counted on the Deity to guide her in living out the implication of her choice.[1] She offered support to her aging relative, with the result that both she and Elizabeth benefitted from their cooperative stance. *Pseudo-Philo*'s Hannah persevered in spite of her own shortcomings and the complex circumstances that were beyond her control. She seized the opportunity to speak, teaching the people how to live and encouraging them to count on rewards after death. All three, as well as the targumic Hannah, overcame tremendous obstacles and served in pivotal ways to improve life for themselves and their descendants. Their determination and their reliance on the Deity offer models for retelling their stories today.

---

1.   Matthew's account describes Mary's situation in more problematic terms than does Luke; see Mt. 1.18–2.23.

BIBLIOGRAPHY

Ackerman, J.S., 'Who Can Stand before YHWH, This Holy God? A Reading of 1 Samuel 1–15', *Prooftexts* 11 (1991), pp. 1-24.

Aejmelaeus, A., 'The Septuagint of 1 Samuel', in *idem* (ed.), *On the Trail of Septuagint Translators* (Kampen: Kok, 1993), pp. 131-49.

Alter, R., *The Art of Biblical Narrative* (New York: Basic Books, 1981).

Amit, Y., ' "Am I Not More Devoted To You Than Ten Sons?" (1 Samuel 1.8): Male and Female Interpretations', in A. Brenner (ed.), *A Feminist Companion to Samuel and Kings* (Sheffield: Sheffield Academic Press, 1994), pp. 68-76.

Bailey, R.C., 'The Redemption of YHWH: A Literary Critical Function of the Songs of Hannah and David', *BibInt* 3 (1995), pp. 213-31.

Berlin, A., *Poetics and Interpretation of Biblical Narrative* (Sheffield: Almond Press, 1983).

Brenner, A., *The Israelite Woman: Social Role and Literary Type in Biblical Narrative* (Sheffield: JSOT Press, 1985).

Brown, R.E., *The Birth of the Messiah: A Commentary on the Infancy Narratives in Matthew and Luke* (Garden City, NY: Doubleday, 1977).

Brueggemann, W., 'I Samuel 1: A Sense of a Beginning', *ZAW* 102 (1990), pp. 33-48.

Callaway, M., *Sing, O Barren One: A Study in Comparative Midrash* (SBLDS, 91; Atlanta: Scholars Press, 1986).

Campbell, A.F., 'Past History and Present Text: The Clash of Classical and Post-Critical Approaches to Biblical Text', *AusBR* 39 (1991), pp. 1-18.

Childs, B., *Introduction to the Old Testament as Scripture* (Philadelphia: Fortress Press, 1979).

Collins, J.J., *The Apocalyptic Imagination: An Introduction to the Jewish Matrix of Christianity* (New York: Crossroad, 1984).

Cook, J.E., 'Females and the Feminine in Pseudo-Philo', in *Proceedings: Eastern Great Lakes and Midwest Biblical Societies* 13 (1993), pp. 151-59.

—'Hannah's Later Songs: A Study in Comparative Methods of Interpretation', in C.A. Evans and J.A. Sanders (eds.), *Early Christian Interpretation of the Scriptures of Israel: Investigation and Proposals* (JSNTSup, 148; SSEJC, 5; Sheffield: Sheffield Academic Press, 1998), pp. 241-61.

—'Pseudo-Philo's Song of Hannah: Testament of a Mother in Israel', *JSP* 9 (1991), pp. 103-114.

—'The Song of Hannah in Pseudo-Philo's *Biblical Antiquities*', in M. Kiley (ed.), *Prayer from Alexander to Constantine: A Critical Anthology* (New York: Routledge, 1997), pp. 73-78.

—'The Song of Hannah: Text and Contexts' (PhD dissertation, Vanderbilt University, 1989).

Cross, F.M., 'The History of the Biblical Text in the Light of the Discoveries in the Judaean Desert', *HTR* 57 (1964), pp. 281-99.

Cross, F.M., and D.N. Freedman, *Studies of Ancient Yahwistic Poetry* (SBLDS, 21; Missoula, MT: Scholars Press, 1975).

Daube, D., *The New Testament and Rabbinic Judaism* (New York: Arno, 1973).

Davis, E.F., 'Swallowing Hard: Reflections on Ezekiel's Dumbness', in J.C. Exum (ed.), *Signs and Wonders: Biblical Texts in Literary Focus* (Semeia Studies; Atlanta, GA: Scholars Press, 1989), pp. 217-37.

Driver, S.R., *Notes on the Hebrew Text and the Topography of the Books of Samuel* (Oxford: Clarendon Press, 2nd edn, 1960).

Dumbrell, W.J., 'The Content and Significance of the Books of Samuel: Their Place and Purpose Within the Former Prophets', *JETS* 33 (1990), pp. 49-62.

Eslinger, L., *Kingship of God in Crisis: A Close Reading of 1 Samuel 1–12* (Bible and Literature Series; Sheffield: Almond Press, 1985).

Exum, J.C., ' "You Shall Let Every Daughter Live": A Study of Exodus 1.8–2.10', in M.A. Tolbert (ed.), *The Bible and Feminist Hermeneutics* (Semeia, 28: Atlanta, GA: Scholars Press, 1983), pp. 63-82.

—'Mother in Israel: A Familiar Story Reconsidered', in L. Russell (ed.), *Feminist Interpretation of the Bible* (Philadelphia: Westminster Press, 1985), pp. 73-85.

Falk, M., 'Reflections on Hannah's Prayer', in C. Buchmann and C. Spiegel (eds.), *Out of the Garden, Women Writers on the Bible* (New York: Fawcett Columbine, 1994), pp. 94-102.

Farris, S., *The Hymns of Luke's Infancy Narratives* (Sheffield: JSOT Press, 1985).

Fitzmyer, J.A., *The Gospel According to Luke I–IX: Introduction, Translation, and Notes* (AB, 28; Garden City, NY: Doubleday, 1981).

Forestell, J.T., 'Old Testament Background of the Magnificat', *Marian Studies* 12 (1961), pp. 205-44.

Freedman, D.N., 'Divine Names and Titles in Early Hebrew Poetry', in *idem* (ed.), *Pottery, Poetry, and Prophecy: Studies in Early Hebrew Poetry* (Winona Lake, IN: Eisenbrauns, 1980), pp. 77-129.

Fuchs, E., 'The Literary Characterization of Mothers and Sexual Politics in the Hebrew Bible', in A.Y. Collins (ed.), *Feminist Perspectives on Biblical Scholarship* (Chico, CA: Scholars Press, 1985), pp. 117-36.

García-Treto, F.O., ' "A Mother's Paean, A Warrior's Dirge": Reflections on the Use of Poetic Inclusions in the Books of Samuel', *Shofar* 11 (1993), pp. 51-64.

Gnuse, R.K., *The Dream Theophany of Samuel* (Lanham, MD: University Press of America, 1984).

Gordon, R.P., 'The Problem of Haplography in 1 and 2 Samuel', in G.J. Brooke and B. Lindars (eds.), *Septuagint, Scrolls and Cognate Writings* (Atlanta: Scholars Press, 1992), pp. 131-58.

—'Who Made the Kingmaker? Reflections on Samuel and the Institution of the Monarchy', in A.R. Millard, J.K. Hoffmeier and D.W. Baker (eds.), *Faith, Tradition, and History: Old Testament Historiography in its Near Eastern Context* (Winona Lake, IN: Eisenbrauns, 1994), pp. 255-69.

Green, J.B., 'The Social Status of Mary in Luke 1.5–2.52: A Plea for Methodological Integration', *Biblia* 73 (1992).

Gunkel, H., 'Die Lieder in der Kindheitsgeschichte Jesu bei Lukas', in *Festgabe A. Von Harnack zum 70. Geburtstag dargebracht* (Tübingen: J.C.B. Mohr, 1921), pp. 43-60.

Harrelson, W., 'Creative Spirit in the Old Testament: A Study of the Last Words of David (2 Sam. 23.1-7)', in D. Durkin, OSB (ed.), *Sin, Salvation, and the Spirit* (Collegeville, MN: Liturgical Press, 1979), pp. 127-33.

Harrington, D.J., 'Pseudo-Philo', *OTP*, II, pp. 297-377.

—'The Apocalypse of Hannah: Targum Jonathan of 1 Samuel 2:1-10', in D.M. Golomb (ed.), *'Working With No Data': Semitic and Egyptian Studies Presented to Thomas O. Lambdin* (Winona Lake, IN: Eisenbrauns, 1987), pp. 147-52.

Harrington, D.J., C. Perrot and P.-M. Bogaert, *Pseudo-Philon: Les Antiquités bibliques*, II (Paris: Cerf, 1976).

Harrington, D.J., and A.J. Saldarini, *Targum Jonathan of the Former Prophets: Introduction, Translation and Notes* (The Aramaic Bible, 10; Wilmington, DE: Michael Glazier, 1987).

Hertzberg, H.W., *I & II Samuel: A Commentary* (OTL; Philadelphia: Westminster Press, 1964).

Horst, P.W. van der, 'Images of Women in the Testament of Job', in M.A. Knibb and P.W. van der Horst (eds.), *Studies on the Testament of Job* (SNTSMS, 66; Cambridge: Cambridge University Press, 1969), pp. 96-106.

—'Portraits of Women in Pseudo-Philo', *JSP* 5 (1989), pp. 29-46.

James, M.R., with Prolegomenon by L.H. Feldman, *The Biblical Antiquities of Philo* (New York: Ktav, 1971).

Jobling, D., 'Hannah's Desire', in D.W. Cotter (ed.), *1 Samuel* (Berit Olam; Collegeville, MN: Liturgical Press, 1998), pp. 131-42.

—'What, If Anything, Is 1 Samuel?', *SJOT* 7 (1993), pp. 17-31.

Johnson, L.T., *The Gospel of Luke* (Sacra Pagina; Collegeville, MN: Liturgical Press, 1991).

Jones, D., 'The Background and Character of the Lukan Psalms', *JTS* 19 (1968), pp. 44-45.

King, K.L., 'Sophia and Christ in the *Apocryphon of John*', in *idem* (ed.), *Images of the Feminine in Gnosticism* (Philadelphia: Fortress Press, 1988), pp. 158-76.

Klein, L.R., 'Hannah: Marginalized Victim and Social Redeemer', in A. Brenner, (ed.), *A Feminist Companion to Samuel and Kings* (Sheffield: Sheffield Academic Press, 1994), pp. 77-92.

Kraemer, R.S., 'Women's Authorship of Jewish and Christian Literature in the Greco–Roman Period', in A.J. Levine (ed.), *'Women Like This': New Perspectives on Jewish Women in the Greco–Roman World* (Atlanta: Scholars Press, 1991), pp. 221-42.

Laffey, A.L., *An Introduction to the Old Testament: A Feminist Perspective* (Philadelphia: Fortress Press, 1988).

Laurentin, R., *Structure et Théologie de Luc I–II* (Paris: Librairie Lecoffre, 1957).

Linafelt, T., 'Taking Women in Samuel: Readers/Responses/Responsibility', in D.N. Fewell, (ed.), *Reading Between Texts: Intertextuality and the Hebrew Bible* (Literary Currents in Biblical Interpretation; Louisville: Westminster/John Knox Press, 1992), pp. 99-113.

Long, V.P., 'Scenic, Succinct, Subtle: An Introduction to the Literary Artistry of 1 & 2 Samuel', *Presbyterion* 19 (1993), pp. 32-47.

Lotto, L., *Annunciation* (Recanati: Pinacoteca Civica c.1534).

Mauchline, J., *1 and 2 Samuel* (NCB; London: Oliphants, 1971).

McCarter, P.K., Jr, *I Samuel: A New Translation with Introduction, Notes and Commentary* (AB, 8; Garden City, NY: Doubleday, 1980).

—'The Books of Samuel', in S.L. McKenzie and M.P. Graham (eds.), *The History of Israel's Traditions: The Heritage of Martin Noth* (Sheffield: Sheffield Academic Press, 1994), pp. 260-80.

McNamara, M., *Targum and Testament: Aramaic Paraphrases of the Hebrew Bible. A Light on the New Testament* (Grand Rapids: Eerdmans, 1972).

Meyers, C., 'The Hannah Narrative in Feminist Perspective', in J. Coleson and V. Matthews (eds.), *Go To the Land I Will Show You* (Winona Lake, IN: Eisenbrauns, 1996), pp. 117-26.

—'An Ethnoarchaeological Analysis of Hannah's Sacrifice', in D.P. Wright, D.N. Freedman and A. Hurvitz (eds.), *Pomegranates and Golden Bells: Studies in Biblical, Jewish, and Near Eastern Ritual, Law, and Literature in Honor of Jacob Milgrom* (Winona Lake, IN: Eisenbrauns, 1995), pp. 77-91.

Murphy, F.J., 'God in Pseudo-Philo', *JJS* 19 (1988), pp. 1-18.

—*Pseudo-Philo: Rewriting the Bible* (New York: Oxford University Press, 1993).

Neusner, J., *What Is Midrash?* (Philadelphia: Fortress Press, 1987).

Nickelsburg, G.W.E., 'Good and Bad Leaders in Pseudo-Philo's *Liber Antiquitatum Biblicarum*', in G.W.E. Nickelsburg and J.J. Collins (eds.), *Ideal Figures in Ancient Judaism: Profiles and Paradigms* (Chico, CA: Scholars Press, 1980).

Ozick, C., 'Hannah and Elkanah: Torah as the Matrix for Feminism', in C. Buchmann, and C. Spiegel (eds.), *Out of the Garden: Women Writers on the Bible* (New York: Fawcett Columbine, 1994), pp. 88-93.

Patrick, D., *The Rendering of God in the Old Testament* (OBT; Philadelphia: Fortress Press, 1981).

Perelmuter, H.G., 'Once a Pun a Preacher', in D. Bergant, and J.T. Pawlikowski (eds.), *Harvest of a Dialogue* (New York: Ktav, 1997), pp. 74-91.

Perrot, C. and P.-M. Bogaert, with the collaboration of D.J. Harrington, *Pseudo-Philon: Les Antiquités bibliques*, I (Paris: Cerf, 1976).

Philonenko, M., 'Une paraphrase du cantique d'Anne', *RHPR* 42 (1962), pp. 157-68.

Polak, F.H., 'Statistics and Textual Filiation: The Case of 4QSam^a/LXX (With a note on the text of the Pentateuch)', in G.J. Brooke, and B. Lindars (eds.), *Septuagint, Scrolls and Cognate Writings* (Atlanta: Scholars Press, 1992), pp. 215-76.

Polzin, R., *Samuel and the Deuteronomist: A Literary Study of the Deuteronomic History Part Two, I Samuel* (New York: Harper & Row, 1989).

Rad, G. von, *Genesis: A Commentary* (OTL; Philadelphia: Westminster Press, rev. edn, 1973).

Reid, B.E., *Choosing the Better Part? Women in the Gospel of Luke* (Collegeville, MN: Liturgical Press, 1996).

Ringe, S.H., *Luke* (Louisville: Westminster /John Knox Press, 1995).

Robertson, D.A., *Linguistic Evidence in Dating Early Hebrew Poetry* (SBLDS, 3; Missoula, MT: Printing Department, University of Montana, 1972).

Schaberg, J., 'Luke', in C.A. Newsom, and S.H. Ringe (eds.), *The Women's Bible Commentary* (Louisville: Westminster/John Knox Press, 1992), pp. 283-84.

Schürmann, H., *Das Lukasevangelium* (Herders theologischer Kommentar zum Neuen Testament, 3.1; Freiburg: Herder, 1969).

Schüssler Fiorenza, E., *Jesus: Miriam's Child, Sophia's Prophet* (New York: Continuum, 1994).

Smith, H.P., *A Critical and Exegetical Commentary on the Books of Samuel* (ICC; Edinburgh: T. & T. Clark, 1899).

Spitta, F., 'Das Magnificat: Ein Psalm der Maria und nicht der Elisabeth', in *Theologische Abhandlung für H.J. Holtzmann* (Tübingen: J.C.B. Mohr, 1902).

Stoebe, H.J., *Das erste Buch Samuelis* (KAT, 8.1; Gütersloh: Gerd Mohn, 1973).

Tannehill, R.C., 'The Magnificat as Poem', *JBL* 93 (1974), pp. 263-75.

—*The Narrative Unity of Luke–Acts: A Literary Interpretation* (Philadelphia: Fortress Press, 1986).

Taylor, B.A., *The Lucianic Manuscripts of 1 Reigns.* I. *Majority Text* (Atlanta: Scholars Press, 1992).

—*The Lucianic Manuscripts of 1 Reigns.* II. *Analysis* (Atlanta: Scholars Press, 1993).

Terrien, S., *The Magnificat: Musicians as Biblical Interpreters* (New York: Paulist Press, 1995).

Trible, P., *God and the Rhetoric of Sexuality* (OBT; Philadelphia: Fortress Press, 1978).

Tsevat, M. 'Was Samuel a Nazirite?', in M. Fishbane and E. Tov (eds.), *'Sha'arei Talmon': Studies in the Bible, Qumran and the Ancient Near East* (Winona Lake, IN: Eisenbrauns, 1992), pp. 199-204.

Walters, S.D., 'Hannah and Anna: The Greek and Hebrew Texts of 1 Samuel 1', *JBL* 107 (1988), pp. 385-412.

Weinfeld, M., *Deuteronomy and the Deuteronomic School* (Oxford: Oxford University Press, 1972).

Weingreen, J., *Introduction to the Critical Study of the Text of the Hebrew Bible* (Oxford: Clarendon Press, 1982).

Wellhausen, J., *Der Text der Bücher Samuelis* (Göttingen: Vandenhoeck & Ruprecht, 1871).

Westermann, C., *Genesis 12–36: A Commentary* (trans. J.J. Scullion; Minneapolis: Augsburg, 1985).

Williams, J.G., *Women Recounted: Narrative Thinking and the God of Israel* (Sheffield: Almond Press, 1982).

Williams, R.J., *Hebrew Syntax: An Outline* (Toronto: University of Toronto Press, 2nd edn, 1976).

INDEXES

INDEX OF REFERENCES

OLD TESTAMENT

INDEX OF AUTHORS

JOURNAL FOR THE STUDY OF THE OLD TESTAMENT
SUPPLEMENT SERIES